INTERMEDIATE LISTENING COMPREHENSION

Understanding and Recalling Spoken English

SECOND EDITION

Patricia Dunkel / Phyllis L. Lim

HEINLE & HEINLE PUBLISHERS

A Division of Wadsworth, Inc.
Boston, Massachusetts 02116 U.S.A.

The publication of *Intermediate Listening Comprehension, Second Edition* was directed by the members of the Newbury House Publishing Team at Heinle & Heinle:

Erik Gundersen, Editorial Director
Susan Mraz, Marketing Manager
Kristin Thalheimer, Production Editor

Also participating in the publication of this program were:

Publisher: Stanley J. Galek
Editorial Production Manager: Elizabeth Holthaus
Project Manager: Angela Malovich Castro, English Language Trainers
Associate Editor: Lynne Telson Barsky
Assistant Editor: Karen P. Hazar
Associate Marketing Manager: Donna Hamilton
Production Assistant: Maryellen Eschmann
Manufacturing Coordinator: Mary Beth Lynch
Interior Designer: Carol H. Rose
Illustrator: Kevin Flynn
Cover Designer: Petra Hausberger

Library of Congress Cataloging-in-Publication Data

Dunkel, Patricia.
    Intermediate listening comprehension: understanding and recalling spoken English / Patricia Dunkel, Phyllis L. Lim.
        p. cm.
    ISBN 0-8384-4838-0
    1. English language—Textbooks for foreign speakers.   2. English language—spoken English.   3. Listening.   I. Lim, Phyllis L.
II. Title.
PE1128.D8273   1993
428.3'4—dc20   93-27953
                                                                                    CIP

Copyright © 1994 by Heinle & Heinle Publishers.

All rights reserved. No part of this publication may be reproduced or transmitted in any form or by any means, electronic or mechanical, including photocopy, recording or any information storage or retrieval system without permission in writing from the publisher.

Heinle & Heinle Publishers is a division of Wadsworth, Inc.

Manufactured in the United States of America

ISBN 0-8384-4838-0

10   9   8   7

CONTENTS

We dedicate this book to the enhancement of intercultural communication and international understanding. We thank all the many students that have contributed to our professional and personal development over the years. Finally, we acknowledge the professional expertise and collegial support of our editor Erik Gundersen.

Overview

Intermediate Listening Comprehension, Second Edition, is an intensive training program in listening fluency development. Over the past fifteen years, there has been a growing interest in and concern for listening training due to the central role listening plays in language development, and communication among people and nations (Dunkel 1991, Rost 1990). The ability to comprehend spoken English can also influence success in the business and academic world for both native speakers of English and those whose native language is other than English. Wolvin and Coakley's (1991) review of 500 major business corporations in the United States indicated that the ability to understand English is the most necessary and important communication skill for the corporations' workers and managers. Wolvin and Coakley were talking about those workers and managers *who speak English as a native language*! The ability to comprehend spoken English has become very important for many nonnative speakers of English to achieve success in business and their academic studies, particularly for those who intend to study in English-speaking universities. When asked to indicate the relative importance of listening, reading, speaking, and writing for international students' success in their academic departments at universities in Canada and the United States, the American and Canadian professors of engineering, psychology, chemistry, computer science, English, and business gave the skills of reading and listening the highest ratings in importance (Wolvin & Coakley, 1991).

In 1981, Nord pointed out that a second language learner must actually have a broader competency in listening comprehension than in speaking, since the listener has little or no control over the vocabulary, speech rate, or content used by the speaker. And yet very few English-as-a-second/foreign-language texts are devoted wholly to listening fluency training. *Intermediate Listening Comprehension, Second Edition,* with its accompanying tape program is directed toward the goal of helping nonnative speakers of English at the intermediate level develop their listening fluency skills. Another aim of *Intermediate Listening Comprehension* is to familiarize the learner with the major rhetorical patterns of formal, spoken English. College-bound students, in particular, need to become acquainted with the cues, structure, and vocabulary indicating that a speaker or lecturer is using one or several of the major rhetorical patterns of speech and thought. In summation, *Intermediate Listening Comprehension* develops the student's listening comprehension by (1) providing samples of clearly enunciated, slow-paced speech as well as more extemporaneous, authentic-sounding extended discourse; (2) teaching recognition of the cue signals of five targeted rhetorical patterns of expository discourse; and (3) providing a variety of task-oriented listening and speaking activities.

Organization of the Program ━━━━━━━━━━━━━━━━━━

Intermediate Listening Comprehension, Second Edition, has five units which focus on the following rhetorical patterns:

> I Chronology
> II Process
> III Definition/Classification
> IV Comparison/Contrast
> V Casual Analysis

Each unit is graded in terms of length and difficulty of grammatical structures used in the talk. Each of the units consists of two to five chapters. Each chapter is organized into three sections:

The Prelistening Task

    A. Listening Preparation
    B. Preview of Vocabulary and Sentences
    C. Rhetorical Listening Cues

The Main Listening Task

    A. Initial Listening
    B. Mental Rehearsal and Review of the Talk
    C. Consolidation

The Postlistening Task

    A. The Comprehension Check
        1. Recognizing Information and Checking Accuracy
        2. Using and Expanding on the Information in the Talk
            a. Recapping the Information From Your Notes
            b. Expanding on the Information in the Talk
    B. The Listening Expansion
    (a variety of listening tasks)
    C. The Listening Factoid

The Instructional Design of Each Chapter ━━━━━━━━━━

The Prelistening Task

    A. Listening Preparation. This initial portion activates the student's world knowledge to help him or her predict the content and course of the discourse. The student is prepared for the talk he or she will hear and is asked to focus on the topic of the discourse. Evocation of mental imagery is attempted in this preparatory stage.

B. Preview of Vocabulary and Sentences. Here, students focus on the low frequency and/or story-specific vocabulary with a gloss and then the item in the talk-specific context.

C. Rhetorical Listening Cues. Finally, this section highlights the specific vocabulary, structures and organization of the particular rhetorical pattern used during the talk.

The Main Listening Task

A. Initial Listening. This section presents the listening passage in its entirety. A natural pace and clear delivery is used by the speaker.

B. Mental Rehearsal and Review of the Talk. Now, the student is provided with the opportunity to review and mentally rehearse the essential message units of the talk. The rehearsal allows for chunking of the information contained in the talk. The student repeats the units subvocally, concentrating on the comprehension and recall of information presented in the talk.

C. Consolidation.* This final segment presents the message units reinserted into the contextual and syntactic whole of the talk. The speaker uses redundancies, reiteration, and verbal fillers in the presentation. Students can take notes during the paced presentation if they wish.

The Postlistening Task

A. The Comprehension Check

   1. Recognizing Information and Checking Accuracy. Here, students check their comprehension and recall of the factual information contained in the talk. The student becomes familiar with standard oral-comprehension testing formats, including multiple choice items, true-false statements, short answer questions, etc.

   2. Using and Expanding on the Information in the Talk
   a. Recapping the Information From Your Notes. This activity offers students the opportunity to recount the information in the talk with the aid of their notes.
   b. Expanding on the Information in the Talk. This portion allows students to interact with other students, expressing their own ideas and opinions on a variety of topics related to the lecture.

B. The Listening Expansion

Tasks 1 and 2 can be completed only by carefully listening to the directions and information given orally. The listening task exercises spiral through previously presented rhetorical patterns, vocabulary, and structures, and also present novel listening and testing experiences.

---

*The script of the Consolidation will vary somewhat from the script of the Initial Listening because of paraphrasing, and inclusion of restarts, verbal fillers, and restatements reflective of more authentic spoken discourse.

C. The Listening Factoid

The Listening Factoid presents a novel, high-interest, sometimes surprising fact related to the topic of the chapter. Students listen to absorb an interesting bit of information or trivia to ponder or discuss as they wish.

Illustrations

Each unit has a general thematic illustration that visually develops the theme of the talk.

Illustrations also accompany many of the vocabulary items and numerous Listening Expansion exercises.

References

Dunkel, P. (1991). Listening in the native and second/foreign language: Toward integration of research and practice. *TESOL Quarterly*, *25*, 431–457.

Nord, J. R. (1981). Three steps leading to listening fluency: A beginning. *The Comprehension Approach to Foreign Language Instruction*, ed. H. Winitz, Rowley, MA: Newbury House.

Rost, M. (1990). *Listening in Language Learning*, New York: Longman.

Wolvin, A., & Coakley, C. (1991). A survey of the status of listening training in some Fortune 500 corporations. *Communication Education*, *40*, 152–164.

INTERMEDIATE LISTENING COMPREHENSION

FOCUS ON

Chronology

Chronology is a way of telling something in the order in which it

happened. Chronology is used to tell stories and to relate historical events.

NAPOLEON
From Schoolboy to Emperor

I. The Prelistening Task

A. Listening Preparation

You are going to listen to a story about Napoleon Bonaparte, the French conqueror. Think about the man for a minute. Do you have a picture of him in your mind? What did he look like? Was he a tall man? No, he was really quite short, but he was a very powerful man. Some people think he was a great man—a hero. Other people think he was a villain—a very bad person. But most people agree that he was one of the most important men in European history.

B. Preview of Vocabulary and Sentences

emperor the ruler of an empire

- Napoleon was a French soldier who became *emperor* of the French Empire.

military school a school that trains young people to be soldiers or officers

- Napoleon's father sent him to *military school* in France.

to excel to do better than others

- Napoleon *excelled* in mathematics and in military science.

career an occupation followed as one's lifework

fame recognition; distinction; great honor

- Napoleon began the military *career* that brought him *fame*, power, riches, and finally defeat.

victories conquests; successes

- Napoleon won many, many military *victories*.

to control to have power over; to govern by domination

- At one time Napoleon *controlled* most of Europe.

to lose to fail to keep; to be unable to save

- In the military campaign into Russia, Napoleon *lost* most of his army.

to be deserted to be left by people who do not plan to return; to be abandoned

- The great French conqueror died alone—*deserted* by his family and his friends.

C. Rhetorical Listening Cues

In this talk the speaker tells you about the life of Napoleon. The story is told in chronological order; that is, the events are related in the order in which they happened. The story begins with Napoleon's birth in 1769 and ends with his death in 1821. Listen for what happened when Napoleon was 10 years old, 16 years old, and 24 years old. Another time expression you will hear that shows chronology is "several years later."

II. The Main Listening Task

A. Initial Listening

Now let's listen to a talk about the Emperor Napoleon. It may help you to concentrate on the talk if you close your eyes while you listen. Just relax and listen carefully.

B. Mental Rehearsal and Review of the Talk

All right. Let's listen to the talk once again. This time, the talk will be given in message units. Please repeat each unit to yourself *silently* after you hear it. Remember, don't say the units out loud.

C. Consolidation

You will hear the talk given once again. This time as you listen, take notes on what you hear.

III. The Postlistening Task

A. The Comprehension Check

1. Recognizing Information and Checking Accuracy

For questions 1–4 you will hear multiple choice questions about the information presented in the talk. Listen to each question and decide whether (a), (b), (c), or (d) is the best answer to the question.

_____ 1. (a) in 1769
    (b) in 1821
    (c) in France
    (d) on Corsica

_____ 2. (a) outstanding
    (b) excellent
    (c) good
    (d) poor

_____ 3. (a) power
    (b) wealth
    (c) defeat
    (d) all of the above

_____ 4. (a) when he was fifty-one years old
    (b) just before he defeated England
    (c) after his military campaign into Russia
    (d) several years after he became a general

For questions 5–8 you will hear statements about the life of Napoleon. If the statement is true, put a T on the line next to the number of the statement. If the statement you hear is false, put an F on the line, and explain why the statement is false.

CHECK YOUR ANSWERS

5. _____ 6. _____ 7. _____ 8. _____

2. Using and Expanding on the Information in the Talk

a. Recapping the Information From Your Notes. Use your notes to recap the information you learned about the life of Napoleon. Present the information to the class or to one of your classmates.

b. Expanding on the Information in the Talk. Discuss with a classmate why you agree (or do not agree) with the following statements:

1. Napoleon was a great man.

2. It would be impossible today for a person like Napoleon to become powerful enough to conquer and rule so many countries.

3. The only way a country can be safe is to have a powerful military to protect itself.

4. Every young man and woman should be required to do at least two years of military service for his or her country.

B. The Listening Expansion

TASK 1.   **Completing a Map**

Look at the map on the following page. It is a picture of the various European kingdoms and empires that existed in Napoleon's time. You are going to fill in the information that is not already on the map. Listen and fill in the missing information.

TASK 2.   **Answering Questions About the Completed Map**

Now the map is complete. Here are some questions about the map of Napoleonic Europe. When you hear a question, look at the map to find the answer to the question you hear. Listen for the words "north," "south," "east," or "west." Write the answer to the question on the appropriate blank line.

For example: You will hear the question: "What was the name of the empire that was south of the Austrian Empire in Napoleon's time?" The answer to the question is "the Ottoman Empire." You must complete the rest of the answers. Are you ready? Do you have the map handy for consultation? Good. Let's begin.

1. _____

2. _____

3. _____

4. _____

5. _____

| CHECK YOUR ANSWERS |

6. _____

LISTENING FACTOID ▶ Napoleon led a very exciting and dangerous life, but he died in his own bed. However, the cause of Napoleon's death has been the subject of controversy from that time to the present. Listen to some of the theories people have had about the cause of his death.

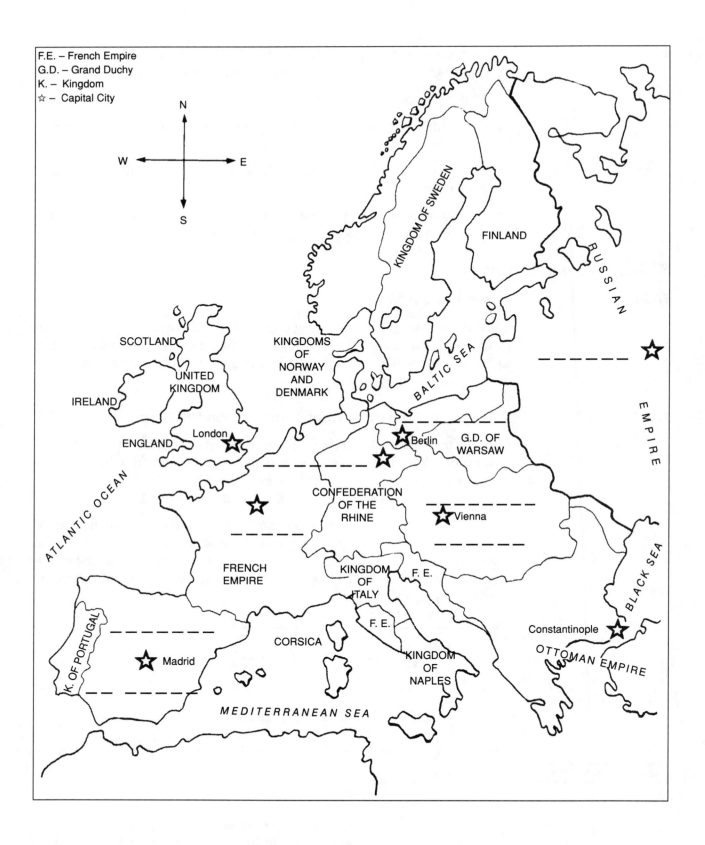

F.E. – French Empire
G.D. – Grand Duchy
K. – Kingdom
☆ – Capital City

N
W — E
S

SCOTLAND

UNITED
KINGDOM

IRELAND

ENGLAND

London ☆

ATLANTIC OCEAN

KINGDOM OF SWEDEN

FINLAND

KINGDOMS
OF
NORWAY
AND
DENMARK

BALTIC SEA

RUSSIAN

☆

EMPIRE

☆ Berlin

G.D. OF
WARSAW

☆

CONFEDERATION
OF THE
RHINE

☆ Vienna

☆

BLACK SEA

FRENCH
EMPIRE

KINGDOM
OF
ITALY

F. E.

F. E.

KINGDOM
OF
NAPLES

Constantinople ☆

OTTOMAN EMPIRE

K. OF PORTUGAL

☆ Madrid

CORSICA

MEDITERRANEAN SEA

POMPEII
Destroyed, Forgotten, and Found

I. The Prelistening Task

A. Listening Preparation

You are going to listen to a story about the ancient city of Pompeii. What do you know about Pompeii? Do you know where it was located? Do you know why it is famous? What happened in Pompeii? Why did many people die there? Why do tourists visit Pompeii today?

B. Preview of Vocabulary and Sentences

Bay of Naples

- Pompeii was located on the ocean, on the *Bay of Naples*.

79 A.D. 79 years after the birth of Christ

- In the year *79 A.D.*, a young Roman boy was visiting his uncle in Pompeii.

sight a scene; a view

- Pliny saw a frightening *sight*.

ash residue left when material is consumed by fire; very small particles of mineral matter that a volcano sends out

- Rock and *ash* flew through the air.

to flee to run to escape from danger

- Many people were able *to flee* the city and to escape death.

to be buried alive to be covered by ash or dirt completely while still living and then to die

- These unlucky people were *buried alive* under the ash.

to dig to turn up the ground or soil with a shovel

- An Italian farmer was *digging* on his farm.

archaeologists scientists who study the remains of ancient civilizations

- *Archaeologists* began to excavate—to dig—in the area.

ruins the remains of destroyed buildings or cities

- Today tourists come from all over the world to see the *ruins* of the famous city of Pompeii.

C. Rhetorical Listening Cues

In this talk the speaker tells you a story about the ancient city of Pompeii. This story begins about 2,000 years ago and continues up to today. The story is told in chronological order. Listen for dates such as "79 A.D." and time expressions such as "for about three days," "as time went by," and "for 1,700 years." These time expressions and dates will help you to understand the sequence or order of events in the story.

II. The Main Listening Task

A. Initial Listening

Now let's listen to a talk about the destroyed city of Pompeii. It may help you to concentrate on the talk if you close your eyes while you listen. Just relax and listen carefully.

B. Mental Rehearsal and Review of the Talk

All right. Let's listen to the talk once again. This time, the talk will be given in message units. Please repeat each unit to yourself *silently* after you hear it. Remember, don't say the units out loud.

C. Consolidation

You will hear the talk given once again. This time as you listen, take notes on what you hear.

III. The Postlistening Task

A. The Comprehension Check

1. Recognizing Information and Checking Accuracy

You will hear five questions about the story. Listen to each question and then write the correct answer to each question in the space provided. Write short answers. (There are several possible answers to some questions.)

1. _____

2. _____

3. _____

4. _____

5. _____

For questions 6–11 you will hear statements about the destruction of Pompeii. If the statement is true, put a T on the line next to the number of the statement. If the statement is false, put an F on the line, and explain why the statement is false.

CHECK YOUR ANSWERS

6. ____   7. ____   8. ____   9. ____   10. ____   11. ____

2. Using and Expanding on the Information in the Talk

a. Recapping the Information From Your Notes.   Use your notes to recap the information you learned about the eruption of the volcano on ancient Pompeii. Present the information to the class or to one of your classmates.

b. Expanding on the Information in the Talk.   Discuss with a classmate the following topics:

1. In your opinion, what is the most dangerous man-made disaster facing the world, and what do you think we can do about it?

2. Describe the worst storm, flood, or natural disaster you (or one of your friends or relatives) ever survived?

3. What should you do to save your life if you find yourself in the following situations?
   (a) You are sitting on a beach on the coast of Indonesia, and suddenly realize that a tidal wave is coming.
   (b) You are visiting Pompeii to see the ruins, and Mr. Vesuvius suddenly erupts with great force.
   (c) You are visiting Miami, Florida, and a hurricane occurs.
   (d) You are visiting Oklahoma, and a tornado strikes the neighborhood you're living in.
   (e) You are staying in a high-rise hotel in San Francisco, and you feel the hotel tremble and shake because a strong earthquake has hit the city.

4. If I am destined to be in a natural disaster, I would prefer a/an

   _____ because _____.

5. Hollywood has made many "disaster" movies, such as *The Towering Inferno,* and *The Poseidon Adventure,* and *Earthquake.* Why do people enjoy watching disaster movies? What is your favorite disaster movie? Why did you enjoy this movie?

B. The Listening Expansion

TASK 1.   **Listening for Sequence Identification**

You will hear two sentences—a pair of sentences. Listen carefully and decide if the sentences are given in the correct time sequence. After you listen to each pair of sentences, write *yes* in the space provided if the sentences are in the correct time sequence. Write *no* if the sentences are not in the correct time sequence. Listen to the following two examples.

Example 1. _____   *Example 2.* _____

Are you ready? The following pairs of sentences are from the story about Pompeii. Think about the time sequence in the story.

1. _____   4. _____

2. _____   5. _____

CHECK YOUR ANSWERS   3. _____   6. _____

TASK 2.   ## Listening to Complete and Use a Chart

You are going to complete the following chart about famous volcanoes. Listen to the short lecture and be ready to fill in the information. Follow the instructions in the lecture. At first, you will just listen and look at the chart. I will tell you when to begin to write the information in the blank spaces on the chart. Are you ready?

Famous Volcanoes of the World			
Name	Location	Date of Eruption	Approximate Number of People Who Died
Vesuvius	Italy	79 A.D.	2,000
Cotopaxi	Ecuador	1877	
Krakatoa	Indonesia		36,000
Mont Pelée	Martinique	1902	
Mount St. Helens	Washington State (U.S.A.)	1980	
Mount Tambora	Indonesia		

Now let's use the chart to list the volcanoes in the order of their eruptions. Find the name of the volcano that erupted first in this group of six volcanoes. Write the name of that volcano next to the number 1. Now write the name of the volcano that erupted next according to the dates on the chart. Continue in this way until you have listed the six volcanoes in the order of their eruptions.

1. _____   4. _____

2. _____   5. _____

CHECK YOUR ANSWERS   3. _____   6. _____

LISTENING FACTOID ▶ Can a volcano shoot down a plane? Listen to this strange happening.

CHAPTER 3

HARRIET TUBMAN

A Conductor on the Underground Railroad

I. The Prelistening Task

A. Listening Preparation

For many years before and during the American Civil War, a young woman of African descent carried a price on her head. She was wanted by authorities in both the North and the South of the United States for helping black slaves escape from their white masters. Her name was Harriet Tubman, but she was better known as Moses. She led more slaves to freedom than any other person, black or white, male or female, in American history. Although her own government never recognized her, the Queen of England, Queen Victoria, who read of her bravery, did. She sent Tubman a silver medal and invited her to come to England. The story of this woman's life and her fight against slavery is the topic of the lecture you will hear.

B. Preview of Vocabulary and Sentences

a plantation a large southern estate or farm on which crops such as cotton and tobacco were grown; black slaves were used as laborers on the plantation

a Maryland plantation a plantation in the state of Maryland in the United States

- Tubman was an African-American who was born in slavery on *a Maryland plantation* in 1820.

to be captured to be taken prisoner; to have one's freedom taken away

- Tubman *was captured* and severely beaten for trying to run away.

an informal network of people a group of people who are not well organized but who have similar interests or goals

- The Underground Railroad was *an informal network of people* in the United States and Canada who believed slavery was wrong.

a runaway slave a slave who escaped from the plantation on which he or she was held in slavery

to give shelter to give someone a safe place to sleep and eat; to give housing and protection to someone in need

- The people of the Underground Railroad helped *runaway slaves* by giving them *shelter* on their journey out of the South.

fugitive slaves a runaway slave who fled from slavery and is being pursued by the authorities

- The members of the Underground Railroad helped hide the runaway or *fugitive* slaves, and then they "conducted" them to the next safe home or "station."

a nurse someone who takes care of the sick and dying

a spy; a commando one who secretly watches and reports on the activities of others; one who obtains secret information and gives it to others

- Tubman served as *a nurse* for the North, but she also served as *a spy* and *a commando*.

a small woman in stature a woman small in size

a giant someone who is very great or large

- Harriet Tubman was *a small woman in stature*, but she was *a giant* in the story of the fight against slavery in the United States.

C. Rhetorical Listening Cues

In this talk the speaker narrates the story of a great heroine of American history, Harriet Tubman. She was called "the Moses of Her Race" because she helped so many slaves escape from slavery. The speaker uses certain words and phrases to tell the chronology of her life, words and phrases such as the following:

> She was born in the year 1820, . . .
> When she was only seven years old, . . .
> In 1849, . . .
> Between 1850 and 1860, . . .
> In 1861, . . .
> Until the American Civil War ended in 1865, . . .
> She lived until 1913.

II. The Main Listening Task

A. Initial Listening

Now let's listen to a talk about a remarkable American who fought against slavery and who helped hundreds of slaves escape to Canada. It may help you to concentrate on the talk if you close your eyes while you listen. Just relax and listen carefully.

B. Mental Rehearsal and Review of the Talk

Let's listen to the talk once more. This time the narrative about Harriet Tubman will be given in message units. Please repeat each of the sentences or phrases to yourself *silently* as you hear it spoken. Remember, do not repeat the units out loud.

C. Consolidation

You will now hear the talk once again. Now that you have an idea of the information contained in the talk, as you listen, take notes on a separate sheet of paper.

III. The Postlistening Task

A. The Comprehension Check

1. Recognizing Information and Checking Accuracy

For questions 1–5, you will hear multiple choice questions about the information presented in the talk. Listen to each question and decide whether (a), (b), (c), or (d) is the best answer to the question asked.

_____ **1.** She _____.
   (a) was severely beaten
   (b) served as a nurse for
       the army
   (c) ran away from the
       plantation
   (d) conducted 300 slaves to
       freedom

_____ **2.** (a) 19
   (b) 150
   (c) 300
   (d) 800

_____ **3.** (a) 1850
   (b) 1860
   (c) 1861
   (d) 1865

_____ **4.** (a) 1861
   (b) 1863
   (c) 1865
   (d) 1913

_____ **5.** (a) commandos
   (b) army scouts
   (c) abolitionists
   (d) Confederates

For questions 6–10, you will hear a statement of fact. If the fact relates to information about Harriet Tubman's story, check the box headed "Harriet Tubman." If the statement concerns another person in history, check the box labeled "Someone in History Other Than HT."

	Harriet Tubman	**Someone in History Other Than Tubman**
6.		
7.		
8.		
9.		
10.		

CHECK YOUR ANSWERS

2. Using and Expanding on the Information in the Talk

a. Recapping the Information From Your Notes.   Use your notes to recap the information you learned about the life and struggle of Harriet Tubman. Present the information to the class or to one of your classmates.

b. Expanding on the Information in the Talk.   Discuss with a classmate the following issues involving slavery, racial prejudice, and intolerance.

1. Slavery takes many forms in today's world. Slavery is not dead.

2. Benjamin Disraeli, former British prime minister, once said, "The difference of race is one of the reasons why I fear war may always exist; because race implies difference, difference implies superiority, and superiority leads to predominance." Is Disraeli right?

3. Martin Luther King, Jr. once spoke of his hopes and dreams for his country, the United States. He said,

   I have a dream that one day this nation will rise up and live out the true meaning of its creed: "We hold these truths to be self-evident that all men are created

equal." ... *I have a dream that my four little children will one day live in a nation where they will not be judged by the color of their skin but by the content of their character. I have a dream today.*

4. What are some of the hopes and dreams you hold for your country?

5. Some forms of prejudice seem "socially acceptable." Bernice Sandler said that sex prejudice is so ingrained in American society that many who practice it are simply unaware that they are hurting women. "It is the last socially acceptable prejudice." Is sex prejudice socially acceptable? If so, why is it so? And is prejudice (1) understandable, and (2) justified under certain circumstances, in certain situations, or in certain societies?

B. The Listening Expansion

TASK 1.

Filling in Information and Answering Questions

You are going to listen to a story about the struggle for civil rights and equality for African-Americans following the U. S. Civil War. As you listen, follow along in your book. While you listen and read, fill in the missing information in the blank spaces.

The Struggle for Equal Civil Rights

At the beginning of the Civil War in _____, there were more than four million African-Americans in the United States. About _____ of these people were enslaved in the South. When the Civil War ended in _____, all the slaves were freed. The Congress of the United States in the next few years passed the _____ and _____ Amendments to the U.S. Constitution to guarantee these newly freed people equal civil rights, including the right to vote. However, Southern states almost immediately began to pass laws which segregated, or separated, black people in schools, public places, and housing. Both legal and illegal ways to prevent these people from voting were also used. Unfortunately, the U.S. Supreme Court in _____ upheld a law in the Southern state of Louisiana which segregated black people on trains. The Supreme Court decided that " _____ _____ _____ " facilities were not against the Constitution. This decision led to about

_____ years of institutionalized segregation in the South. Although segregation was never legal in the North, there was still widespread discrimination, and segregation in schools and housing was quite common. During _____ things began to change and by the end of the war, the military was completely desegregated. That is, segregation was ended in the military. During the _____ and _____, more and more states began to pass laws against segregation and discrimination, and in _____, the Supreme Court reversed its earlier "separate but equal" decision and decided that "separate but equal" facilities violated people's civil rights. The Supreme Court ordered that public schools be desegregated. In 1964 Congress passed the Civil Rights Act, which outlawed discrimination in public facilities, public education, labor unions, and employment. The Voting Rights Act, passed in _____, helped to protect every person's right to vote. This brief outline of the struggle for equal civil rights emphasized the legal side of the struggle. The human side of the struggle is, of course, dramatic and moving, with great determination and courage shown by leaders and common people together.

From the information you have filled in, answer the following questions. Write short answers. Listen carefully to the question.

1. _____

2. _____

3. _____

4. _____

CHECK YOUR ANSWERS

5. _____

TASK 2.

Reading to Put Sentences Into Chronological Order

The following sentences about famous civil rights leader Martin Luther King are not a good paragraph. They are out of correct order. Read all of the sentences one time to get a general idea of the main ideas of the paragraph. When you finish, read the directions following the sentences.

Martin Luther King, 1929–1968

A. He followed in his father's footsteps as a Baptist minister, but he also became the most influential leader of the civil rights movement of the 1950s and 1960s, organizing nonviolent protests against discrimination.

B. Probably the next most important historical event he was involved in was the March on Washington for Jobs and Freedom, where he gave his famous "I Have a Dream" speech in August of 1963.

C. She was arrested for refusing to move to the back of the bus as the law required.

D. Congress passed the 1964 Civil Rights Act the next year.

E. Following her arrest, Dr. King organized a successful black boycott of the buses.

F. The success of the bus boycott showed how powerful the strategy of nonviolent resistance could be and increased his stature as a national leader for civil rights.

G. One of the most important events that he was involved in began in December, 1955, when a black woman, Rosa Lee Parks, was arrested in Montgomery, Alabama.

H. Martin Luther King was born in the Deep South, in Atlanta, Georgia, in 1929, the son of a Baptist minister.

I. Although King had preached nonviolence as a way of life, he was assassinated in 1968, and his death sparked riots in more than 100 cities.

J. The same year that the Civil Rights Act was passed, Martin Luther King was awarded the Nobel Peace Prize.

Now, after having read the jumbled sentences, arrange them in the correct chronological order. Place the letter of the sentences on the blank lines. For example, the first sentence in the story is "H," "Martin Luther King was born in Atlanta, Georgia, in 1929, the son of a Baptist minister." Two other sentences have been done to help you. Now go on with the others.

1. _H_   6. _____

2. _____   7. _____

3. _____   8. _____

4. _____   9. _____

CHECK YOUR ANSWERS   5. _E_   10. _I_

Now retell the entire story in your own words.

LISTENING FACTOID ▶ Although the North had fought to free the South's slaves, after the war, Tubman and other former slaves discovered that Northerners could be as prejudiced as Southerners. Listen to what happened to Harriet Tubman when she was riding on a railroad, a *real* railroad, one time.

UNIT TWO

Process

Process tells how to do something, how something works, or how something happens (for example, how children acquire language).

CHAPTER 1

JET PROPULSION
How It Works in Principle

fig. 1

fig. 2

fig. 3

Fig. 4

I. The Prelistening Task

A. Listening Preparation

What happens when you release a balloon filled with air? It flies all around the room. The balloon is pushed forward by the air that escapes from the balloon. Well, the engine of a jet plane and the engine of a rocket work on a similar principle. The jet plane and the rocket are pushed forward by the backward escaping of gas from the plane and the rocket. In the rocket, fuel is ignited (set on fire). As the fuel burns, it generates a high-pressure gas (see figure 1). The gas pushes out in all directions inside the rocket, as illustrated in figure 2. When the rocket's exhaust is opened, the hot gas rushes out. The rush of the gas out of the rocket pushes it forward (see figure 3) and up into the air, in the case of the jet plane (see figure 4). You can better understand how jet propulsion works by conducting your own simple experiment. In this talk you will learn how to make a rocket boat. If you were going to do this experiment, you would need the following items:

> 1 aluminum tube with a twist-off top (lid)
> 1 nail
> 1 hammer
> 2 pipe cleaners
> 3 small candles
> 1 aluminum tray
> glue
> water

B. Preview of Vocabulary and Sentences

power-driven flight of a plane the flight of a plane driven by the burning of a fuel; the flight of a plane other than a glider

- The first *power-driven flight of a plane* occurred in 1903 when Orville Wright flew his plane for a distance of 120 feet at an air speed of 30 miles per hour.

ton 2,000 pounds in the United States and Canada; in Britain, 2,240 pounds

- How does a plane weighing 85 *tons* ever get into the air?

jet propulsion a method of moving a plane, rocket, or other vehicle in one direction by using a stream or "jet" of hot gas forced out in the opposite direction

- *Jet propulsion* puts the plane into the air.

hollow having a hole or empty space inside; not solid

- You will need a *hollow* aluminum tube.

to twist on and off to turn to open and to close

- The tube needs to have a lid or top that can be *twisted on and off.*

to punch a hole in to make a hole or opening in

- Take the aluminum tube and *punch a hole in* its top or lid.

a jet of exhaust steam the used steam that escapes from the opening in the hollow, water-filled tube

- The boat will be thrust forward by *a jet of exhaust steam.*

C. Rhetorical Listening Cues

In this talk, the speaker describes how to make a rocket boat to illustrate how forward thrust (propulsion) works. The speaker uses certain words and phrases to show the order, or the sequence, of the events described. The speaker uses words and phrases such as the following:

First, . . .
Then, . . .
Next, . . .
The next thing you need to do . . . .
Now, . . .
After that, . . .

II. The Main Listening Task

A. Initial Listening

Now let's listen to a talk about how to make a rocket boat. Look at the illustration of the process as you listen to the talk.

B. Mental Rehearsal and Review of the Talk

Let's listen to the talk once more. This time the description of the process will be given in message units. Please repeat each of the sentences or phrases to yourself *silently* as you hear it spoken. Remember, do not repeat the units out loud.

C. Consolidation

You will now hear the talk once again. Now that you have an idea of the information contained in the talk, as you listen, take notes on a separate sheet of paper on the process.

III. The Postlistening Task

A. The Comprehension Check

1. Recognizing Information and Checking Accuracy

For questions 1–4, you will hear multiple choice questions about the information presented in the talk. Listen to each question and decide whether (a), (b), (c), or (d) is the best answer to the question asked.

_____ **1.** (a) 12 seconds
    (b) 8–12 feet
    (c) 85 tons
    (d) 400 people

_____ **3.** (a) glue
    (b) water
    (c) candles
    (d) jet exhaust

_____ **2.** in the _____
    (a) lid
    (b) candles
    (c) pipe cleaners
    (d) aluminum tray

_____ **4.** (a) the water heats up
    (b) the lid is replaced
    (c) the candles are lighted
    (d) the rocket boat moves
       forward

For questions 5–8, you will hear statements about the rocket boat experiment. If the statement is true, put a T on the line next to the number of the statement. If the statement you hear is false, put an F on the line, and explain why the statement is false.

CHECK YOUR ANSWERS

5. ____   6. ____   7. ____   8. ____

2. Using and Expanding on the Information in the Talk

a. Recapping the Information From Your Notes.   Use your notes to recap the information you learned about how to make a rocket boat. Present the information to the class or to one of your classmates.

b. Expanding on the Information in the Talk

(1) Explaining a Principle: The Egg in the Bottle

The principle behind the hot air balloon is the same as the principle behind the egg in the bottle.

Look at the illustration of the egg in a bottle demonstration below. The experiment illustrates how the hot air balloon works. It demonstrates that when air is heated, it expands (it gets larger in volume), and when it cools, it contracts (it gets smaller in volume) again. Earlier you heard a description of an experiment to demonstrate the principle of rocket thrust. Now, it's your turn to explain a demonstration from the illustration below. In other words, tell what happens to the egg and the bottle experiment. Be sure to include some rhetorical cues in your description.

(2) Discussion: Discuss with a classmate why you agree (or do not agree) with the following statements:

1. One day, people will be flying to other planets, and this will be a good thing for humankind.

2. Flying today is safe and comfortable for all the passengers. I do not think we need all the security that is in place at airports.

3. Rockets can be used for good or bad purposes.

4. In the future, people will be able to fly to the planets when more powerful rockets are developed. This will be a good thing for future peoples of the world.

B. The Listening Expansion

TASK 1.   **Connecting the Processes**

Listen to the following description of a space flight to another planet. The description begins with the preparation for the flight and ends with the astronauts preparing to return to earth. Fill in the missing transitional cues.

A flight to another planet such as Mars might follow a schedule like this:

_____ a target planet will be selected and _____,
  (1)   (2)
it will be photographed and carefully mapped. The rocket carrying

the spacecraft with the astronauts in it will be prepared for the voyage.

_____, the men and women astronauts will be selected and
  (3)
trained for the flight. When everything is ready, the rocket will blast off

from earth. _____, the rocket will dock at an orbiting space
              (4)
station in order to refuel. _____, it will blast off from the
                              (5)
space station and head toward the target planet. The trip will be long.

_____, the spacecraft will enter the target planet's orbit.
  (6)

_____, it will make a soft landing on the planet.
  (7)

_____ the astronauts will leave the spaceship and explore
  (8)
the planet. _____ they will reenter their mother ship and
              (9)
begin their preparations for the trip back to earth.

CHECK YOUR ANSWERS

TASK 2.

Testing Your ESP

One of the astronauts who flew to the moon in Apollo 14 tried to communicate telepathically with friends on earth. In other words, he tried to send his thoughts to his friends on earth. Telepathy is one kind of extrasensory perception (ESP). Russian scientists have also tried similar telepathy experiments on earth. Here's an experiment that you can try with a friend to test each other's ESP, or psychic ability. Listen to the explanation, and then try the experiment with a friend.

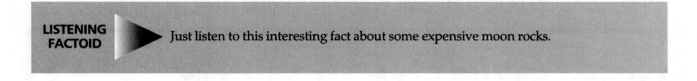

LISTENING FACTOID Just listen to this interesting fact about some expensive moon rocks.

CHAPTER 2

LANGUAGE
How Children Acquire Theirs

I. The Prelistening Task

A. Listening Preparation

How do babies communicate before they know how to speak any language? When do they begin to make language-like sounds? Are these first language-like sounds the same for all babies, or do babies from different language backgrounds make different sounds? At what age do they begin to say their first words? What does it mean that children's first sentences are "telegraphic"? What kinds of grammar mistakes do children make when learning their own language? You will learn the answers to these questions when you listen to the talk on how children acquire their language.

B. Preview of Vocabulary and Sentences

cooing noises soft and gentle sounds like the sounds a pigeon makes

- The first stage begins in a few weeks when they start to make *cooing noises* when they are happy.

to babble to make and play with meaningless sounds like "goo-goo-goo" and "da-da-da"

- Around four months of age babies begin *to babble*.

to invent words to create their own special words

- These first words are *words* that they *invent* for themselves, for example, a baby may say "baba" for the word "bottle," or "kiki" for "cat."

to acquire words to learn words

- In the next few months, the baby will *acquire* quite a few *words* and begin to use them to communicate with others.

telegraphic in the style of a telegram, that is, expressed in as short a way as possible

essential basic; necessary; required

- This language is often called *telegraphic* because the baby omits all except the most *essential* words.

to overgeneralize to use a rule too freely; to use a rule where it doesn't fit

- They also begin to *overgeneralize* these basic rules, and, as a result, they make a lot of mistakes.

C. Rhetorical Listening Cues

In this talk the speaker discusses how children acquire language. The speaker uses certain words and phrases to show the order, or the sequence, of the process. The speaker uses words and phrases such as these:

As soon as . . .
At first . . .
The first stage . . .
The next stage . . .

II. The Main Listening Task

A. Initial Listening

Now let's listen to a talk about how children acquire language. It may help you to concentrate on the talk if you close your eyes while you listen. Just relax and listen carefully.

B. Mental Rehearsal and Review of the Talk

Let's listen to the talk once more. This time the description of how children acquire language will be given in message units. Please repeat each of the sentences or phrases to yourself *silently* as you hear it spoken. Remember, do not repeat the units out loud.

C. Consolidation

You will now hear the talk once again. Now that you have an idea of the information contained in the talk, as you listen, take notes on what you learn about the process of language acquisition.

III. The Postlistening Task

A. The Comprehension Check

1. Recognizing Information and Checking Accuracy

For questions 1–3 you will hear multiple choice questions about the information presented in the talk. Listen to each question and decide whether (a), (b), (c), or (d) is the best answer to the question.

_____ 1. at _____
    (a) birth
    (b) 4 months
    (c) 10 months
    (d) 18 months

_____ 2. (a) "kiki"
    (b) "Daddy up"
    (c) "I went home."
    (d) "I goed sleep."

_____ 3. (a) 10–12 months
    (b) 18–24 months
    (c) 2–3 years
    (d) 7–8 years

For questions 4–7 you will hear statements about how children acquire language. If the statement is true, put a T on the line next to the number of the statement. If the statement you hear is false, put an F on the line.

CHECK YOUR ANSWERS

4. _____   5. _____   6. _____   7. _____

2. Using and Expanding on the Information in the Talk

a. Recapping Information from Your Notes. Use your notes to recap the information you learned about how children acquire language. Present the information to the class or to one of your classmates.

b. Expanding on the Information in the Talk. Discuss with a classmate why you agree (or do not agree) with the following statements:

1. It is very confusing for a baby to have to learn two languages at the same time, so parents who speak two different languages should agree to speak only one language to the child.

2. It's important for parents to talk to their babies a lot to help them learn their language.

3. Some languages are more difficult for babies to learn than other languages.

4. It's easy for a baby to learn his or her language, but it's hard work for an adult to learn a second language.

5. Babies would not learn to talk if nobody spoke to them.

6. All people who live in a country should be able to speak at least one common language.

7. It would be better if everybody in the world spoke the same language.

8. Some languages are better for science, some for poetry, and others for romance and love.

B. The Listening Expansion

TASK 1.

Solving a Word Problem

You are going to listen to a problem that needs to be solved. Look at the picture as you listen to the problem. After you listen to the problem, discuss it with a partner to be sure you both understand the nature of the problem. Then work together to try to solve the problem. Now, listen to the problem.

When you think you have a solution, find another pair of students who have also solved the problem. Take turns explaining the process you used in finding a solution to the problem. For example, "First, we tried . . . . After that, we . . . . Next, we . . . . Finally, ... "

TASK 2.

Explaining Steps in Problem Solving

You will need a piece of paper and three coins of different sizes to solve the following problem. When you are ready, listen to the problem. When you have listened to the problem, discuss the problem with a partner to be sure you both understand the nature of the problem. Then work on the problem until you solve it.

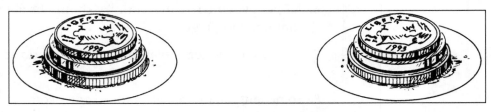

After you have solved the problem, write out the steps that must be followed in order to solve this problem. Begin this way, "First, move the (name of coin) to . . . . Next, ..." Continue until you have listed every step necessary to solve the problem.

LISTENING FACTOID ▶ Listen to the story of an ancient experiment to discover what language children would speak if they never heard anyone speaking their language.

CHAPTER 3

HYDROPONIC AQUACULTURE
How One System Works

I. The Prelistening Task

A. Listening Preparation

There are many countries and places in the world that lack three essential commodities: vegetables, fish, and water, according to a recent article in *The Arizona Daily Star* newspaper. However, scientists have developed a simple but effective method of producing these three commodities. They can produce fish and vegetables in water using hydroponic aquaculture. How do they do this? First, the scientists collect rainwater in a tank. They then raise fish in the rainwater collected, and, finally, they grow vegetables on the waste from the fish raised in the rainwater. How can fish and vegetables be raised in an aquaculture (or hydroponic) environment? Let me tell you how one hydroponic process functions. I'll describe an aquaculture experiment that raises fish and vegetables on the Island of St. Croix.

B. Preview of Vocabulary and Sentences

gravity the force that pulls things toward the center of the earth; the force that causes objects to fall when they are dropped

recirculating water systems systems that make water complete a full cycle and then start the process all over again

- The system uses *gravity* to create *recirculating water systems.*

tank a large container that holds liquids such as water

- Rainwater is collected in a large 3,000 gallon *tank.*

waste from the fish the food not digested by the fish and eliminated from the body by the fish

- The other tank holds the *waste from the fish.*

to be filtered to be made clean and pure

- After the water *is filtered,* it is passed through a bio-filter that contains bacteria.

tray a raised, flat surface that is used to hold items (such as plants)

- Just above the 100-foot long tanks of water, lettuce plants are suspended on *trays.*

to soak up (to absorb) to take in and make a part of itself

nutrient an element in food that is needed by people, animals, and plants for life and growth

- The plants *soak up* or *absorb* the nitrates and other *nutrients* in the water.

pump a machine that is used to move water and other liquids or a gas from one place to another place

- A *pump* is used to cycle the water back up to the 3,000 gallon fish tank.

profitable money making

- A commercial company would need to have several tanks in order to make the process *profitable.*

C. Rhetorical Listening Cues

In this talk the speaker discusses how one system of hydroponic aquaculture works. The speaker uses certain words and phrases to show the order, or the sequence, of the process described. The speaker uses words and phrases such as the following:

> To start, . . .
> Once the tank is filled, . . .
> First, . . .
> Then, . . .
> Subsequently, . . .
> The next step in the process, . . .
> After it is filtered, . . .
> It is now necessary to . . .

II. The Main Listening Task

A. Initial Listening

Now let's listen to a talk about a hydroponic experiment to raise fish and lettuce plants. Look at the illustration of the process as you listen to the talk.

B. Mental Rehearsal and Review of the Talk

Let's listen to the talk once more. This time the description of the aquaculture process will be given in message units. Please repeat each of the sentences or phrases to yourself *silently* as you hear it spoken. Remember, do not repeat the units out loud.

C. Consolidation

You will now hear the talk once again. Now that you have an idea of the information contained in the talk, as you listen, take notes on a separate sheet of paper on the process.

III. The Postlistening Task

A. The Comprehension Check

1. Recognizing Information and Checking Accuracy

For questions 1–3, you will hear multiple choice questions about the information presented in the talk. Listen to each question and decide whether (a), (b), (c), or (d) is the best answer to the question asked.

_____ 1. (a) bacteria
     (b) nitrates
     (c) filtering
     (d) gravity

_____ **2.** (a) bacteria
(b) nitrates
(c) filtering
(d) gravity

_____ **3.** (a) 1,000
(b) 3,000
(c) 10,000
(d) 25,000

For questions 4–7, you will hear statements about hydroponic aquaculture. If the statement is true, put a T on the line next to the number of the statement. If the statement is false, put an F on the line and explain why the statement is false.

CHECK YOUR ANSWERS

4. _____   **5.** _____   **6.** _____   **7.** _____

2. Using and Expanding on the Information in the Talk

a. Recapping the Information From Your Notes. Use your notes to recap the information you learned about the hydroponic system of growing lettuce. Present the information to the class or to one of your classmates.

b. Expanding on the Information in the Talk. Discuss with a classmate why you agree (or do not agree) with the following statements:

1. Hydroponic aquaculture would be a cost-effective and efficient method of growing food in my country.

2. Many things could go wrong with hydroponic aquaculture.

3. Developing countries would benefit more using aquaculture than would developed countries.

4. I would prefer to eat vegetables grown in soil than in the hydroponic environment.

5. Some people eat to live; others live to eat. I live to eat.

6. If the following foods were prepared and served for dinner at a friend's house, I would eat:

horse meat	elephant meat
snake meat	octopus
grasshoppers and	
crickets	the eyes of an animal
raw fish	the brains of an animal
roast dog	the heart and intestines of
monkey meat	an animal
pork	
camel meat	mushrooms a friend found in the
kangaroo meat	woods near his house

B. The Listening Expansion

TASK 1.   **Listening to Identify Steps**

You are going to listen to steps that can be followed to achieve a yoga position. First look at the seven pictures below. These pictures are the steps necessary to do the yoga exercise. However, they are not in the correct order. You must listen carefully and number the pictures. (Notice that two of the pictures are the same, but you will need both of them in order to complete the steps.)

Now that you have completed putting the pictures in correct order, you could try out the yoga exercise. Don't worry if you can't do it perfectly. Just move as far as is comfortable for you. Never do anything that hurts or makes you uncomfortable.

TASK 2.   **Taking Your Pulse**

People who exercise vigorously, for example, people who run, ride a bicycle, or do other aerobic exercises are often interested in knowing what their pulse rate is before and after they exercise. Taking your pulse is easy. Listen to the steps. You may want to take brief notes.

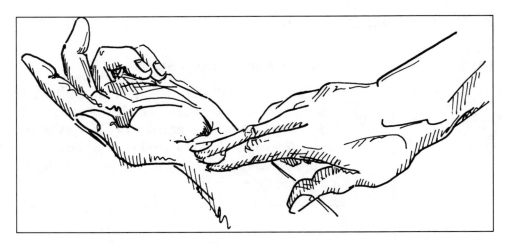

Practice explaining these steps to a partner. Then take your pulse and write

the number here. pulse rate _____

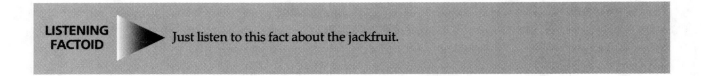

Just listen to this fact about the jackfruit.

UNIT THREE

FOCUS ON
Classification/ Definition

Classification is a way of putting people, places, things or ideas into groups, or classes. All of the items in one class have something in common. The classes are separate and complete, and are often organized by physical features or uses. Definition is a way of first describing how something is a member of a general class (genus) and then how the subject is different from all others of that class.

THE NEWS MEDIA
Print Media and Electronic Media

I. The Prelistening Task

A. Listening Preparation

How do you find out what's happening in the world every day? Do you listen to the radio? Do you watch the news on television? The news media tell us what is happening in our city, in our country, and in the world. You are going to listen to a talk about the various kinds of news media.

B. Preview of Vocabulary and Sentences

category a class or division
- The news media can be classified into two general *categories*.

air waves forms of electrical energy that travel through the air from one point to another
- Electronic media use *air waves* to send news into homes, offices, and public places.

to publish to print and make available to the public
- The newspaper *The New York Times* is *published* once a day.

for instance for example
- *For instance, Newsweek* and *Time* magazines are published once a week.

to broadcast to send programs over radio or television
- In the United States, many radio stations *broadcast* five minutes of news every hour on the hour.

to develop to grow; to increase
- In the future, new categories of news media will *develop*.

to influence to have an effect on

transmission sending from one place to another

reception receiving
- Computers are beginning to *influence* the *transmission* and *reception* of news.

events occurrences

computer users people who have and use computers for a variety of reasons
- Many *computer users* in the United States were able to receive information about *events* happening in other parts of the world from computer users in those parts of the world.

BITNET and INTERNET computer networks that allow computer users to "talk" to one another via electronic mail
- The users transmitted news via electronic mail over computer networks like *BITNET and INTERNET*.

C. Rhetorical Listening Cues

In this talk the speaker classifies the news media into two main categories: print news media and electronic news media. The speaker gives examples of items in each of the two categories. In which of the two categories do you think radio news belongs? Radio news is an example of electronic news media. During the talk you will hear the speaker use words that indicate categorization of the media. You will hear phrases such as "are divided into" and "are classified into." Are you ready?

II. The Main Listening Task

A. Initial Listening

Now let's listen to a classification of the two categories of news media: print media and electronic media. It may help you to concentrate on the talk if you close your eyes while you listen. Just relax and listen carefully.

B. Mental Rehearsal and Review of the Talk

Let's listen to the talk once again. This time, the talk will be broken down into message units. Please repeat each of the sentences or phrases to yourself *silently* after you hear it. Remember, do not repeat the units out loud.

C. Consolidation

You will now hear the talk given once again. Now that you are familiar with the information contained in the talk, try to take notes while you are listening to the speaker.

III. The Postlistening Task

A. The Comprehension Check

1. Recognizing Information and Checking Accuracy

For questions 1–6, you will hear multiple choice questions about the information presented in the talk. Listen to each question and decide whether (a), (b), (c), or (d) is the best answer to the question asked.

_____ 1. (a) TV
    (b) radio
    (c) air waves
    (d) newspapers

_____ 2. (a) air waves
    (b) magazines
    (c) newspapers
    (d) all of the above

_____ 3. (a) magazine
    (b) newspaper
    (c) radio program
    (d) television program

_____ 4. (a) *Newsweek*
    (b) *Time*
    (c) *The New York Times*
    (d) all of the above

_____ 5. (a) TV programs
    (b) newspapers
    (c) magazines
    (d) none of the above

_____ 6. (a) 15,000 plus
    (b) 11,000 plus
    (c) 1,500 plus
    (d) 1,100 plus

For questions 7–12, you will hear statements about print and electronic media. If the statement is true, put a T on the line next to the number of the statement. If the statement is false, put an F on the line, and explain why the statement is false.

CHECK YOUR ANSWERS

7. ____ 8. ____ 9. ____ 10. ____ 11. ____ 12. ____

2. Using and Expanding on the Information in the Talk

a. Recapping the Information From Your Notes. Use your notes to recap the information you learned about the news media. Present the information to the class or to one of your classmates.

b. Expanding on the Information in the Talk. Discuss with a classmate the following issues involving the news media.

1. News is always presented in a factual and objective manner by those who write the news stories.

2. News about an event or situation that is broadcast in one country might appear very different from the news about the same event or situation in another country.

3. Our country is portrayed badly by the news media in other countries

   such as _____. Explain why.

4. My favorite TV program is _____ because

   _____.

5. The kind of news that fascinates me is stories about _____

   _____ because _____.

6. Rank order the programs listed below according to your preference for viewing them, and explain your reasons for your ranking to a classmate.

   ____ (a) soap operas

   ____ (b) weekly news programs

   ____ (c) game shows

   ____ (d) daily news programs

   ____ (e) sitcoms (situation comedies)

   ____ (f) dramas

   ____ (g) quiz shows

   ____ (h) entertainment specials

_____ (i) MTV programs

_____ (j) old movies

_____ (k) new movies

7. What did the famous Canadian communications scholar Marshall McLuhan mean when he said the following:
   a. "The medium is the message."
   b. "The new electronic independence recreates the world in the image of a global village."

B. The Listening Expansion

TASK 1.   **Identifying Different Segments of a News Broadcast**

The radio news broadcast is made up of several different segments:

 There's the *international* news—information from around the world.

 There's the *national* news—information about events within the country.

 There's the *local* news—information about what is happening in and around the city or area in which the listener lives.

 There's *sports* news—information about baseball, football, tennis, etc.

 There's a report about the *weather*.

 There are also sometimes *commercials*—advertisements for products or services.

In this exercise you are going to listen to six excerpts from a news broadcast. Listen to each part of the news broadcast and decide which kind of news the announcer is giving.

For example: You will hear "Today was cool and cloudy with a high of 62 degrees Fahrenheit. Tonight's low will be in the low 30s. So get out our warm blankets, and turn up the heat."

Question: What kind of news report is this?

The announcer was giving a *weather report;* so you would write the word "weather" on the blank line next to 1. Let's continue.

1. _____   4. _____

2. _____   5. _____

CHECK YOUR ANSWERS

3. _____   6. _____

TASK 2.

Rating Restaurants

You will overhear conversations in four different restaurants. The diners are talking about the quality of the food served and the cost of the meal. Listen to each conversation and categorize the food as good or bad. Use the couple's comments on the food and the cost to make your decision about the quality and cost of the food in the four restaurants.

For example: You will hear

RALPH: How did you enjoy the fish, dear?

ANNE: Well, it was . . . uhm . . . a little overdone, to tell the truth.

RALPH: My steak was tough. And the dessert was nothing special. For the prices they charge here, I certainly expected a much better meal.

ANNE: So did I. Let's not come here again.

The diners did not enjoy the food because the fish was so-so and the food was expensive. For restaurant 1, therefore, check the boxes labeled "Bad Food," and "Expensive Prices." Let's go on.

	Food		Prices	
Restaurant	Good	Bad	Expensive	Inexpensive
1		✔	✔	
2				
3				
4				

CHECK YOUR ANSWERS

LISTENING FACTOID What program do you think most Americans watch on a weekly basis? Is it a soap opera? Is it a sitcom? Is it a game show? Listen to this interesting factoid from the *1993 Universal Almanac.*

CHAPTER 2

A TIDAL WAVE

What Is It? What Causes It? How Can We Predict it?

I. The Prelistening Task

A. Listening Preparation

Look at the picture. A tidal wave is about to strike the city. Tidal waves are one of the great forces of nature. Tidal waves can be very dangerous to people. They have caused a lot of destruction to property, and they have killed many people. What exactly is a tidal wave? What causes a tidal wave? How can we predict when a tidal wave will strike? Do you know the answers to these questions? Listen and find out the answers to these questions. "What exactly is a tidal wave?" "What causes a tidal wave?" "How can we predict when a tidal wave will strike?"

B. Preview of Vocabulary Sentences

destructive damaging; ruinous

to rush to move forward very quickly; to speed
- A tidal wave is a very large and *destructive* wall of water that *rushes* in from the ocean toward the shore.

storms heavy, windy rainfalls or snowfalls
- Do you know that tidal waves are not caused by *storms?*

to shift to change position
- When a seaquake takes place at the bottom of the ocean, the ocean floor shakes end trembles and sometimes *shifts.*

to predict to tell in advance; to foretell
- Today scientists can *predict* when a tidal wave will hit land.

to warn to advise of coming danger
- It is possible to *warn* people that a tidal wave is coming.

C. Rhetorical Listening Clues

In this talk you will hear several definitions given. In other words, the speaker will explain the meanings of some of the words or expressions. Sometimes the speaker will explain an expression by telling you what it is. For example, you will hear, "A tidal wave is a very large and very destructive wave that rushes in from the ocean like a huge tide." And sometimes you will hear the speaker explain a word or expression by telling you what it is not. For example, you will hear, "Tidal waves are not true tides." This is an example of a *negative* definition. Sometimes the speaker will give you a synonym for a word. Then again the speaker will explain a word by breaking it down into its parts. For example, the word "seaquake" is made up of two words: "sea" and "quake." The speaker will explain the meaning of *both* words. You will hear the speaker define the following word or words: "tidal wave," "true tide," "seaquake," "to quake," and "seismograph."

II. The Main Listening Task

A. Initial Listening

Now let's listen to a talk about what a tidal wave is, what causes a tidal wave, and how a tidal wave can be predicted by scientists. It may help you to concentrate on the talk if you close your eyes while you listen. Just relax and listen carefully.

B. Mental Rehearsal and Review of the Talk

All right. Let's listen to the talk once again. This time, the talk will be given in message units. Please repeat each unit to yourself *silently* after you hear it. Remember, don't say the units out loud.

C. Consolidation

You will now hear the whole talk once again. This time as you listen, take a few notes on what you hear.

III. The Postlistening Task

A. The Comprehension Check

1. Recognizing Information and Checking Accuracy

Are you ready for a quiz on the story? Column A contains six blank lines. Column B lists some words and phrases from the story. Look over the information in Column B. O.K. Here's what you have to do. First, you will listen to a statement. Then you should look at the choices listed in Column B. Match the correct choice with the statement you hear. For example: Look at 1 in Column A. Statement 1 is "In Japanese it means 'storm wave'." The correct match to the statement, "In Japanese it means 'storm wave' " is choice a—*tsunami*. Put the letter a on line 1. Are you ready to do some more? We'll start with statement 2.

Column A	Column B
____ 1.	a. tsunami
____ 2.	b. seaquake
____ 3.	c. scientists
____ 4.	d. tidal wave
____ 5.	e. ocean floor
____ 6.	f. a seismograph
	g. earthquake
	h. Richter scale

CHECK YOUR ANSWERS

2. Using and Expanding on the Information in the Talk

a. Recapping the Information From Your Notes.   Use your notes to recap the information you learned about *tsunamis*. Present the information to the class or to one of your classmates.

b. Expanding on the Information in the Talk.   Discuss with a classmate the following issues:

1. Natural disasters threaten many populations throughout the world, but natural disasters are not the only or most frightening disasters people face. Diseases like AIDS might put an end to humankind one day.

2. Natural disasters like *tsunamis* cannot be prevented, but we can do something about the spread of AIDS. What can we do to prevent the

spread of AIDS, tuberculosis, and the other contagious diseases that are on the increase?

3. Life expectancy has increased in most countries of the world. Why?

4. How long would you like to live? Why?

5. Many countries still have very low life expectancy. Why? What can be done to help increase the life expectancy of people in these countries?

6. The worst kind of natural disaster is _____ because

_____.

B. The Listening Expansion

TASK 1.

Filling In Information and Answering Questions

In this exercise you will complete a crossword puzzle using words from the story. Some of the words will be written across and some of the words will be written down. When two words meet or cross each other, they will share a common letter. For example, number 1 across and number 1 down both begin with the same letter. Let's do number 1 across together. Are you ready? Number 1 across: It's a word with 11 letters. It's an instrument that records information about an earthquake. The word is "seismograph." Write the word "seismograph" beginning in box 1 and continuing across to box 11. Seismograph is spelled s-e-i-s-m-o-g-r-a-p-h. Are you ready to complete the puzzle? I will tell you how many letters each word has and give you a definition of the word. You may not know how to spell each word. Just do your best. Let's begin.

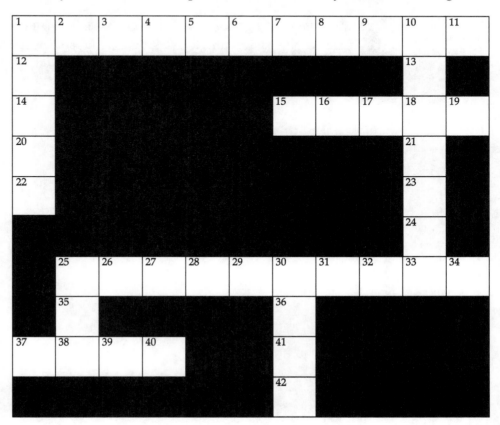

CHECK YOUR ANSWERS

Catching and Correcting Mistakes in Information

In this exercise you will listen to a brief news report about a tidal wave that struck Japan several years ago. Like all news reports, this report is full of factual information. Factual information contains the names of places, dates, numbers, or happenings. After you listen to the report, you will read five statements about the tidal wave. You will check the accuracy of some statements made about the event, about the tidal wave, by catching the error and correcting the sentence.

Now listen carefully to the news report of the event that happened on May 26, 1983, in northwestern Japan. Ready?

Now read the following statements related to the news report you just heard. Each statement contains one error or one incorrect piece of information. Correct the mistake by restating the sentence correctly. For example, you will read: "An earthquake struck the northeastern coast of Japan." You will say: "An earthquake struck the *northwestern* coast of Japan."

1. Fifteen people were caught in the tidal wave.

2. The tidal wave hit the coast an hour after the earthquake.

3. A 20-foot-high wave struck the beach.

4. The quake caused widespread destruction of beaches.

5. The President of the United States declared a state of emergency.

LISTENING FACTOID

On August 27, 1883, the volcanic island of Krakatoa blew up. Some 36,000 people were killed by the *tsunamis* that followed the eruption and the earthquake, but do you know that the largest wave known was not a *tsunami*? Listen.

ACID RAIN
A Growing Hazard to the Environment

I. The Prelistening Task

A. Listening Preparation

Today in parts of Europe and North America rainwater is sometimes more acidic than lemon juice. You have probably heard the term *acid rain* and know about the serious damage acid rain has already caused to the environment. You may have heard that one of the most famous forests in the world, the Black Forest in Germany, is seriously threatened by acid rain and that some lakes have "died" because of acid rain. We know that acid rain is not only causing damage to nature, it is even causing damage to many old buildings, statues, and historical monuments. The speaker today is going to tell you about acid rain and will tell you what acid rain is and will tell you some upsetting facts about acid rain.

B. Preview of Vocabulary and Sentences

historical monuments a building or other kind of structure built in memory of an historical event such as a war

- Imagine *historical monuments* being destroyed by rainwater.

slightly acidic not very, but somewhat acidic

- Ordinary rainwater is *slightly acidic.*

to dissolve to break down into parts and become part of a fluid such as water

- When these gases *dissolve* in rainwater, they make the water somewhat acidic.

fossil fuels energy sources which are formed from the remains of ancient plants and animals

- The most important cause of acid rain is the burning of *fossil fuels* such as petroleum and coal.

combine with to join with; to become part of

- These gases *combine with* water molecules and form acid.

water droplets very small drops of water

- These acidic water *droplets* then can travel hundreds of miles before they return to earth as rain or snow.

competition a situation in which people try to get or win things of which there is a limited supply

- As more and more countries become industrialized, there will be more and more *competition* for the fossil fuels.

to contribute to have part of the responsibility for something

- Burning petroleum *contributes* to acid rain.

supply amount of something available for use

to run out to be used up completely

- The *supply* of petroleum will eventually *run out.*

pressure strong demand or influence

- There will be more and more *pressure* to burn coal.

destructive harmful or damaging

- We already know how *destructive* acid rain is.

C. Rhetorical Listening Cues

In this talk the speaker first defines exactly what *acid rain* is. When defining acid rain, the speaker uses these words and phrases:

> The term (acid rain) refers to . . .
> This definition . . .
> In scientific terms, . . . is defined as . . . .

II. The Main Listening Task

A. Initial Listening

Now let's listen to a talk about what acid rain is. It may help you to concentrate on the talk if you close your eyes while you listen. Just relax and listen carefully.

B. Mental Rehearsal and Review of the Talk

Let's listen to the talk once more. This time the definition of acid rain will be given in message units. Please repeat each of the sentences or phrases to yourself *silently* as you hear it spoken. Remember, do not repeat the units out loud.

C. Consolidation

You will now hear the talk once again. Now that you have an idea of the information contained in the talk, as you listen, take notes on the definition.

III. The Postlistening Task

A. Comprehension Check

1. Recognizing Information and Checking Accuracy

For questions 1–4 you will hear multiple choice questions about the information presented in the talk. Listen to each question and decide whether (a), (b), (c), or (d) is the best answer to the question.

_____ **1.** as _____
  (a) acidic
  (b) neutral
  (c) alkaline
  (d) lemon juice

_____ **2.** (a) 7
  (b) 5.5
  (c) less than 5.5
  (d) more than 5.5

_____ **3.** as _____
  (a) rainwater as acidic as lemon juice
  (b) rainwater more acidic than lemon juice
  (c) rainwater more acidic than normal rainwater
  (d) precipitation with a pH of less than 5.5

_____ **4.** (a) carbon dioxide
  (b) nitrogen oxide
  (c) sulfur dioxide
  (d) a, b, & c

For questions 5–8 you will hear statements about the lecture on acid rain. If the statement is true, put a T on the line next to the number of the statement. If it is false, put F on the line, and explain why the statement is false.

CHECK YOUR ANSWERS

5. ____   6. ____   7. ____   8. ____

2. Using and Expanding on the Information in the Talk

a. Recapping the Information From Your Notes.   Use your notes to recap the information you learned about how to define acid rain. Present the information to the class or to one of your classmates.

b. Expanding on the Information in the Talk.   Discuss with a classmate why you agree (or do not agree) with the following statements:

1. There should be an international law that no country can burn coal.

2. Human beings are more important than the environment, so we shouldn't worry about the environment but about how to see that everyone in the world has what he or she needs and wants.

3. I would be willing to give up my car if everybody else did in order to help solve the acid rain problem.

4. Ordinary people can't do much about this kind of problem. We should leave it up to the government to solve this problem.

5. Rich, industrialized countries are mostly to blame for most environmental problems, so other countries shouldn't worry about these kinds of problems.

B. The Listening Expansion

TASK 1.   **Reconstructing Acronyms and Initialisms**

Acronyms and initialisms are very common in English. You probably have seen and heard them already and perhaps have already used some. Acronyms are words that are formed from the first letters of words in a phrase. For example, the word "laser" is an acronym for *l*ight *a*mplification by *s*timulated *e*mission of *r*adiation. Notice that acronyms are pronounced as words. Initialisms are very similar to acronyms, but initialisms are not pronounced as words. Instead, each letter in an initialism is pronounced as a letter. For example, IBM is an initialism for a famous company called *I*nternational *B*usiness *M*achines. Notice we say I . . . B . . . M. Now you will listen to nine acronyms and initialisms being pronounced. Put an A in the space provided if you hear an acronym and an I if you hear an initialism. Then write down exactly what the letters of the acronym or initialism stand for. For example, for number 1 you will hear "Thank God it's Friday." You will write I for initialism and then write on the line following T.G.I.F. "Thank God it's Friday." You will hear each phrase read three times. You may not be able to spell every word correctly. Just do your best and learn to spell the words you didn't know for homework after you check your answers.

____ **1.** T.G.I.F._____

____ **2.** WHO _____

____ **3.** UFO _____

____ **4.** EPA _____

____ **5.** GNP _____

____ **6.** OPEC _____

____ **7.** NASA _____

____ **8.** ESP _____

____ **9.** AIDS _____

Now match each acronym or initialism with the definition, description, or explanation which best matches it. Write the number of the acronym or initialism next to the letter of the best answer. For example, "Thank God it's Friday" matches letter e.

____ **a.** the ability to know things without using the normal means of knowing such as sight, hearing, touch, or smell

____ **b.** a U.S. government agency whose job is to control and reduce pollution of air and water as well as regulate solid-waste disposal and the use of pesticides, radiation, and toxic substances

____ **c.** an organization of petroleum-producing countries whose purpose is to determine amount of production and to set prices on the petroleum sold to other countries

____ **d.** a United Nations agency which concerns itself with proper food supply and nutrition, safe water and sanitation, maternal and child health, immunization against major infectious diseases, and prevention and control of local diseases in different countries around the world

____ **e.** an expression of gratitude that the work week is almost over and that the weekend is about to begin

____ **f.** the total dollar value of all final goods and services currently produced in an economy as measured by market prices

____ **g.** a U.S. governmental agency that develops, constructs, tests, and operates vehicles for in-flight research within and outside earth's atmosphere

____ **h.** the technical term for what are popularly known as "flying saucers" and believed by some people to be spaceships manned by creatures from other planets such as Mars or Venus

CHECK YOUR ANSWERS

____ **i.** the name for a group of diseases that are found worldwide in people infected by a virus called HIV (human immunodeficiency virus)

TASK 2.   **Listening to Match a Question with Its Answer**

The following answers need questions. Listen while I read a question and find its answer. Write the question on the line before the answer. For example, you will hear "What is the Eiffel Tower?" You should write the question on the line just before answer number 3. Take a minute to look over each answer. Underline a few key words. For example, for answer number 3 the key words might be *structure*, *tall*, and *skyline of Paris*. You will hear each question three times. Don't forget to use a capital letter to begin the first word of the question and a question mark at the end of each question.

1. *Question:* _____

   Answer: An extremely creative and productive person although totally deaf by the time he was in his late 40s, this composer of some of the most famous and intense works is still heard all over the world.

2. *Question:* _____

   Answer: A spectacular gorge cut by the Colorado River in northwest Arizona. It is more than 200 miles long, four to eighteen miles wide, and up to one mile deep. It contains colorful layers of rock dating back more than two million years. About two million people visit it each year.

3. *Question:* _____

   Answer: A famous structure built as the focal point of the Universal Exposition of 1889. It is 984 feet tall. It dominates the skyline of Paris.

4. *Question:* _____

   Answer: A staple food of hundreds of millions of people. It needs hot, moist conditions to grow.

5. *Question:* _____

   Answer: Structures built by ancient people as royal tombs or temples. The first one was built around the year 2650 B.C. The largest one ever built was 482 feet high and covered 13 acres. These structures are found in Egypt and in Central and South America.

6. *Question:* _____

   Answer: The main cereal crop in the world. It grows best in temperate regions of Europe, North America, China, and Australia. It is used to make bread and pasta.

7. *Question:* _____

   Answer: A person of enormous energy and creative imagination, inventor of many of the things we take for granted in everyday life, such as the phonograph and the electric light bulb. He said genius was "1 percent inspiration and 99 percent perspiration."

8. *Question:* _____

   Answer: A world-famous person who lived to be over 90 years old and was creative and productive all of his life. He was a sculptor, graphic artist, ceramist, in addition to his most famous skill. He died in 1973.

9. *Question:* _____

   Answer: A colossal bronze female figure reaching more than 300 feet in height. It was designed by a French architect and given to the U.S. on the 100th anniversary of U.S. independence. It is visited by tourists to New York City.

10. *Question:* _____

    Answer: The most important U.S. crop. It was cultivated in the Americas long before the arrival of Europeans. It is now grown extensively over most of the world. It is an important crop for both humans and animals.

CHECK YOUR ANSWERS

LISTENING FACTOID   Now listen to a talk about how much pollution different machines cause.

LEVELS OF LANGUAGE USAGE
Formal and Informal

I. The Prelistening Task

A. Listening Preparation

Have you ever said something in English and had someone look at you in surprise, laugh at you, or even look at you with uncomprehending eyes? You might have thought you had made a mistake in English grammar or used the wrong word or phrase. However, maybe you didn't make a grammar or vocabulary mistake. It's possible to use English that is appropriate in one situation but that is not appropriate in another situation. Learning a language means not only learning a new grammar and a lot of new words and phrases, but it also means learning how to choose appropriate words and expressions for the situation you are in.

B. Preview of Vocabulary and Sentences

reference books books where one can look up factual information, usually arranged by alphabet, topics, or dates

- Formal written language is found in *reference books* such as encyclopedias.

ceremonies formal activities associated with special occasions

- You will hear formal language at *ceremonies* such as graduations.

to tend to to be likely or inclined to

- We *tend to* use spoken formal language in conversations with persons we don't know well.

colleagues fellow workers in a profession; professional equals

- Informal language is used in conversation with *colleagues*, family and friends.

diaries daily written records of what we do, think, or feel, usually kept private

- Informal language is also used when we write personal notes or letters to close friends, as well as in *diaries*.

in authority in a position of power over other people

- I would use formal English with a stranger or someone *in authority*.

teammates fellow members of a team, usually a sports team

- Classmates, *teammates*, family members, friends, etc., will generally speak in an informal fashion.

interacting entering into relationships, social or professional

- The difference between formal and informal usage can be learned by observing and *interacting* with native speakers.

C. Rhetorical Listening Cues

In this talk the speaker classifies Standard English into two broad categories, or levels, of language usage: formal English and informal English. The speaker gives examples of where each of these levels of English should be used and then gives examples of sentences in both formal and informal English.

II. The Main Listening Task

A. Initial Listening

Now let's listen to a talk about formal and informal levels of English usage. It may help you to concentrate on the talk if you close your eyes while you listen. Just relax and listen carefully.

B. Mental Rehearsal and Review of the Talk

Let's listen to the talk once more. This time the description of the levels of English usage will be given in message units. Please repeat each of the sentences or phrases to yourself *silently* as you hear it spoken. Remember, do not repeat the units out loud.

C. Consolidation

You will now hear the talk once again. Now that you have an idea of the information contained in the talk, as you listen, take notes on the process.

III. The Postlistening Task

A. The Comprehension Check

1. Recognizing Information and Checking Accuracy

For questions 1–4 you will hear multiple choice questions about the information presented in the talk. Listen to each question and decide whether (a), (b), (c), or (d) is the best answer to the question.

_____ **1.** (a) diaries
(b) compositions
(c) personal notes
(d) letters to friends

_____ **2.** (a) family
(b) friends
(c) teammates
(d) a, b, & c

_____ **3.** (a) Salt, please.
(b) Pass the salt.
(c) Pass the salt, please.
(d) Could you please pass the salt?

_____ **4.** (a) I enjoy music.
(b) I saw the cops.
(c) I like Greek food.
(d) none of the above

For questions 5–8 you will hear statements about levels of English usage. If the statement is true, put a T on the line next to the number of the statement. If the statement you hear is false, put an F on the line, and explain why the statement is false.

| CHECK YOUR ANSWERS |

5. _____   6. _____   7. _____   8. _____

2. Using and Expanding on the Information in the Talk

a. Recapping the Information From Your Notes. Use your notes to recap the information you learned about formal and informal levels of English usage. Present the information to the class or to one of your classmates.

b. Expanding on the Information in the Talk. Discuss with a classmate why you agree (or do not agree) with the following statements:

1. It would be better to speak formal English for all situations.

2. It's too difficult for second language learners to learn the difference between formal and informal English. Only native speakers can learn the difference.

3. If a person is not sure which language level to use, it's better to use formal English instead of informal English.

4. Children should be spoken to in informal language.

5. The way a person speaks tells you a lot about that person.

6. English teachers do not teach students how to use informal English, and this causes problems for second language learners.

B. The Listening Expansion

TASK 1. **Labeling the Parts of an Ancient Calculator**

You are going to hear about an ancient calculator called an *abacus*. You will hear a definition of what an abacus is and then will label its parts.

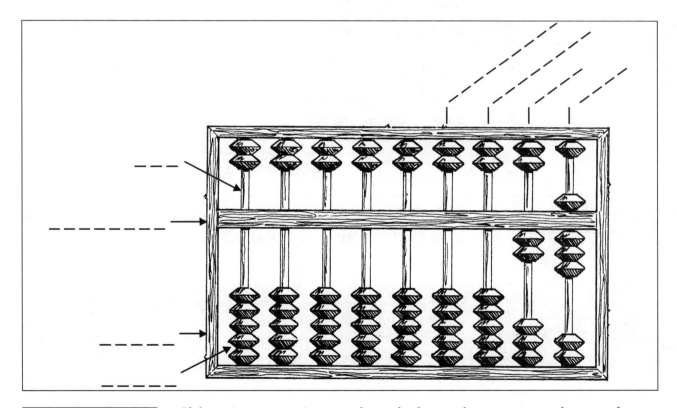

CHECK YOUR ANSWERS If there is someone in your class who knows how to use an abacus, ask your classmate to do a few arithmetic problems to show you how quickly and accurately arithmetic calculations can be made.

Labeling Parts of a Modern Calculator

Modern calculators will do a lot more than the ancient abacus. The abacus is a manual calculator, while modern calculators are electronic. These modern electronic calculators still do the same arithmetic computations that the abacus does, but they also do a variety of other calculations. Today you will label the parts of this fairly simple, modern electronic calculator.

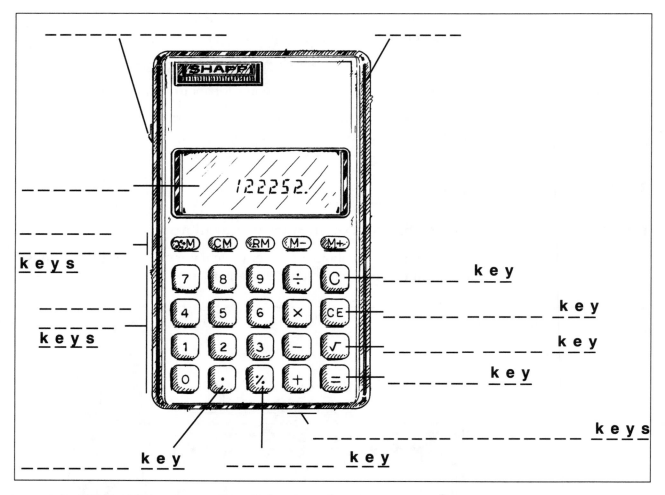

keys

keys

keys

k e y

key

k e y

k e y

k e y

k e y

k e y s

If there is anyone in your class who knows how to use the memory keys, ask your classmate to explain the purpose and use of these keys.

LISTENING FACTOID ▶ A good English-English dictionary can be helpful in determining the level of usage of words as well as help you with spelling, pronunciation, and the meanings of words. For example, many dictionaries will tell you if a word is *informal.* Listen to a short talk about the very long time it can take to prepare a comprehensive dictionary.

CHAPTER 5

POWER
The Kinds People Use and Abuse

I. The Prelistening Task

A. Listening Preparation

What is *power*? When you think of power, what do you think of? Money? Strength? Politics? The social psychologist Edwards defines power as *the ability to determine or to change the actions of other people*. What kinds of power do people use to influence the actions or *behavior* of other people? According to Edwards, they use five basic kinds of power: (1) information power; (2) referent power; (3) legitimate power; (4) expert power; and (5) reward and coercive (or punishment) power. In this talk, I will briefly describe each of these five classifications of power, and I'll give you some examples to illustrate a few of the types.

B. Preview of Vocabulary and Sentences

behavior the way a person acts day after day or at any one time

- Psychologists define power as the ability to determine, or to change the actions or *behavior* of other people.

to manipulate other people to control other people in unfair or dishonest ways

for evil purposes for reasons that are bad or harmful to a person

- Psychologists are trying to understand how people *manipulate* other people for good and *evil purposes*.

to be in a position of power to have the authority to control or direct the actions of other people

- The person who has information that other people want and need, but do not have, is in *a position of power*.

one's own sense of power a person's feeling of personal control and influence over other people and events

- Most people like to receive and have information. Having information increases a person's *sense of power*.

accuracy correctness

- Many readers do not question the *accuracy* of the reports about world events they read in the newspapers.

to imitate the actions of certain people to try to act the way certain other people act and behave

- Referent power results from the desire of people to be like certain other people or *to imitate the actions of certain people*.

to identify with a person to admire and to feel similar to a person

- If you *identify with another person*, that person has power over you and can influence your actions and behavior.

to commit suicide to kill oneself

- In the 1970s in Jonestown, Guyana, more than 900 people *committed suicide* when their religious leader Jim Jones told them to kill themselves.

Waco, Texas a small city in central Texas, in the United States

- More recently, a man named David Koresh controlled the lives and destinies of a small community of men, women, and children in *Waco, Texas*.

a civilian a person who is not in the army, police, etc.

a guard a person who protects someone or something from danger

- In this experiment, a researcher asked people on the street to move away from a bus stop. When he was dressed as *a civilian*, few people moved away from the bus stop. When the researcher was dressed as *a guard*, most people moved away from the bus stop.

to be impressed by to have strong positive feelings about

- Most people are *impressed by* the skills or knowledge of experts.

a chance for gain an opportunity to benefit or be helped

- Giving a reward will change people's behavior because it offers people *a chance for gain*.

C. Rhetorical Listening Cues

In this talk, the speaker classifies various kinds of power. She begins by defining power, and she then goes on to discuss the different types of power. She uses words and phrases which indicate that she is classifying the various kinds of power, and is giving the order or sequence in which they are being discussed; she uses words such as "classify," "is classified," and expressions such as "the first type of power," "the third kind," and so forth.

II. The Main Listening Task

A. Initial Listening

Now listen to a talk about the basic forms of power. Look at the listing on page 61 as you listen to the classification of the different types of power.

B. Mental Rehearsal and Review of the Talk

Let's listen to the talk once more. This time the classification of the various kinds of power will be given in message units. Please repeat each of the sentences or phrases to yourself *silently* as you hear it spoken. Remember, do not repeat the units out loud.

C. Consolidation

You will now hear the talk once again. Now that you have an idea of the information contained in the talk, as you listen, take notes on a separate sheet of paper on the process.

III. The Postlistening Task

A. The Comprehension Check

1. Recognizing Information and Checking Accuracy

For questions 1–3, you will hear multiple choice questions about the information presented in the talk. Listen to each question and decide whether (a), (b), (c), or (d) is the best answer to the question asked.

_____ **1.** (a) reward
     (b) referent
     (c) legitimate
     (d) information

_____ **3.** (a) coercive
     (b) referent
     (c) legitimate
     (d) information

_____ **2.** (a) reward
     (b) referent
     (c) legitimate
     (d) information

For questions 4–9, you will hear statements about ideas. If the speaker mentioned the idea in the talk, put a check in the box "*I heard this idea in the talk.*" If, however, the idea was not mentioned in the talk, but you could infer the idea from the information given in the talk, put a check in the box, "*I didn't hear this idea but can infer it from the information given.*" Finally, if the idea you hear was not mentioned, and could not be inferred from the talk, check the box "*I did not hear this idea in the talk and cannot infer it from the information given.*"

	I heard this idea in the talk	I didn't hear this idea but can infer it from the information given	I did not hear this idea in the talk and cannot infer it from the information given
4.			
5.			
6.			
7.			
8.			
9.			

CHECK YOUR ANSWERS

Now, you create four statements about the talk yourself. Ask a classmate to listen to the statements and to complete the chart below

	I heard this idea in the talk	I didn't hear this idea but can infer it from the information given	I did not hear this idea in the talk and cannot infer it from the information given
10.			
11.			
12.			
13.			

2. Using and Expanding on the Information in the Talk

a. Recapping the Information From Your Notes. Use your notes to recap the information you learned about the five basic kinds of power. Present the information to the class or to one of your classmates.

b. Expanding on the Information in the Talk. Discuss with a classmate why you agree (or do not agree) with the following statements:

1. To some people, power is a game in which winners are powerful, and losers are powerless.

2. There's a saying, "It's a man's world." Because it's a man's world, men have and use power, and women have little or no power.

3. Winning a war is the major sign of the power of a country.

4. Referent power is useful to rock and movie stars, generals in the army, religious leaders, and parents.

5. There are more than five basic kinds of power.

6. Information power is the most effective type of power.

7. Governments that use coercive power over their people generally use the coercive power for good purposes.

8. According to Ralph Waldo Emerson, "You shall have joy or you shall have power, said God; you shall not have both."

B. The Listening Expansion

TASK 1. **Naming the Animal and Naming the Category**

All animals can be grouped according to whether or not they have a back-bone, which is sometimes called a spinal column. Animals that have a spinal column are called "vertebrates." Animals that do not have a spinal column are called "invertebrates." A human being has a spinal column; so she or he is classed as a "vertebrate." A bee has no spinal column. It is classed as an "invertebrate."

In this exercise you will listen to a description of a vertebrate animal or an invertebrate animal. You must first identify the animal described, and then you must categorize the animal as vertebrate or invertebrate by underlining the term "vertebrate" or "invertebrate."

Let's do 1 together.

Listen to the following description. Look at the pictures of the animals.

1. Its a(n) _____. It's classed as a vertebrate/invertebrate.

2. Its a(n) _____. It's categorized as a vertebrate/invertebrate.

3. Its a(n) _____. It's designated as a vertebrate/invertebrate.

4. Its a(n) _____. It's typed as a vertebrate/invertebrate.

5. Its a(n) _____. It's classified as a vertebrate/invertebrate.

6. Its a(n) _____. It's classed as a vertebrate/invertebrate.

7. Its a(n) _____. It's categorized as a vertebrate/invertebrate.

CHECK YOUR ANSWERS

Bee

no backbone
(no spinal
column)

Dinosaur

backbone
(spinal
column)

fly	octopus	frog
owl	horse	shark
tuna	alligator	spider
snake	clam	human being
butterfly	elephant	parrot
whale	salamander	oyster

TASK 2.   **The Five Categories of Vertebrates: Placing the Animal in the Category**

All vertebrate animals are divided into five general categories: mammals, fish, birds, reptiles, and amphibians. In this exercise, you will listen to and read definitions of each vertebrate category. After all the definitions have been given, you will use the information you heard to identify members of each category. Now follow along as the speaker explains what a mammal is. Listen carefully. The explanation is very general.

1. A *mammal* is a warm-blooded vertebrate that feeds its young with milk from the mother's body.

2. A *bird* is a warm-blooded vertebrate that has feathers and two feet. Instead of arms, a bird has wings.

3. A *fish* is a cold-blooded vertebrate that lives its entire life in water. It has fins instead of arms or feet. It gets oxygen from the water, not air.

4. A *reptile* is a cold-blooded vertebrate that crawls or moves on its stomach or on small short legs. Reptile babies hatch from eggs with shells.

5. An *amphibian* is a cold-blooded vertebrate that starts its life in water. Later, an amphibian develops lungs to breathe air. Then it can live on land.

Now you know the five categories of vertebrate animals. You will now hear the name of an animal. It may be a mammal, a bird, a fish, a reptile, or an amphibian. Listen for the name of the animal, and then write the name you hear on the blank line next to the correct number. Then write the category that the animal belongs to.

Animal	Category
1. _____	_____
2. _____	_____
3. _____	_____
4. _____	_____
5. _____	_____
6. _____	_____
7. _____	_____
8. _____	_____
9. _____	_____
10. _____	_____

CHECK YOUR ANSWERS

LISTENING FACTOID 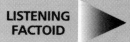 Listen to this fact about a king who was so powerful he was afraid someone would try to poison him.

FOCUS ON

Comparison/ Contrast

Comparison/contrast is a way of showing how people, places, things, ideas, or events are similar or different. Comparison describes the similarities between two or more things. Contrast describes the differences.

CHAPTER 1

ASIAN AND AFRICAN ELEPHANTS
Similarities and Differences

I. The Prelistening Task

A. Listening Preparation

Elephants are fascinating animals. Almost everyone has seen an elephant in a zoo, in a circus, or, at least, in a picture. Tell me, what do you think of when you hear the word "elephant"? Do you know that there are two kinds of elephants? There's the African elephant and there's the Asian, or Indian elephant. The African and the Asian elephants are alike, but they are also very different in many ways. First, let's find out how they are similar, and then let's learn about how they are different. In other words, we are going to compare the African and the Asian elephants to see how they are alike. Then we are going to contrast these elephants to see how the African and the Asian elephants differ from one another.

B. Preview of Vocabulary and Sentences

enormous very large; huge; gigantic
- Elephants are really *enormous* animals.

trunks the long, round, muscular noses of elephants
- Both animals have long noses, called *trunks*.

to train to teach; to instruct
- Both animals can be *trained* to do heavy work.

trick a clever act, intended to amuse or puzzle
- Elephants can also be trained to do *tricks* to entertain people.

temperament personality; disposition; character
- The last big difference between the elephants is their *temperament*.

C. Rhetorical Listening Cues

In this talk the speaker compares and contrasts elephants. The speaker uses words that show similarity, words like "both" and "similarly." You will also hear words and phrases that show differences, words or phrases like "on the other hand," "in contrast," "but," "bigger than," and "more difficult than." These cues will tell you whether the speaker is comparing or contrasting two things—in this case two *big* animals.

II. The Main Listening Talk

A. Initial Listening

Now let's listen to a talk about the similarities and differences between Asian and African elephants. It may help you to concentrate on the talk if you close your eyes while you listen. Just relax and listen carefully.

B. Mental Rehearsal and Review of the Talk

All right. Let's listen to the talk once again. This time, the talk will be given in message units. Please repeat each unit to yourself *silently* after you hear it. Remember, don't say the units out loud.

C. Consolidation

You will listen to the talk once again. This time as you listen, you may want to take a few notes on what you hear.

III. The Postlistening Task

A. The Comprehension Check

1. Recognizing Information and Checking Accuracy

For questions 1–5 you will hear multiple choice questions about the information presented in the talk. Listen to each question and decide whether (a), (b), (c), or (d) is the best answer to the question.

_____ 1. It's the elephant's _____.
    (a) ear
    (b) nose
    (c) tooth
    (d) tusk

_____ 2. (a) African elephants
    (b) Asian elephants
    (c) both of the above
    (d) neither of the above

_____ 3. _____ pounds
    (a) 7,000 to 12,000
    (b) 8,000 to 10,000
    (c) 12,000 to 14,000
    (d) 18,000 to 20,000

_____ 4. It is _____.
    (a) lighter and smaller
    (b) heavier and larger
    (c) smaller and heavier
    (d) larger and lighter

_____ 5. Both _____.
    (a) weigh the same
    (b) have a similar color
    (c) are similar in size
    (d) can learn tricks to entertain people

For questions 6–10, you will hear five statements about ideas. If the speaker mentioned the idea in the talk, put a check in the box "_I heard this idea in the talk._" If, however, the idea was not mentioned in the talk, but you could _infer_ the idea from the information given in the talk, put a check in the box, "_I didn't hear this idea but can infer it from the information given._" Finally, if the idea you hear was not mentioned, and could not be inferred from the talk, check the box "_I did not hear this idea in the talk and cannot infer it from the information given._"

	I heard this idea in the talk	I didn't hear this idea but can infer it from the information given	I did not hear this idea in the talk and cannot infer it from the information given
6.			
7.			
8.			
9.			
10.			

CHECK YOUR ANSWERS

Now, you create four statements about the talk yourself. Ask a classmate to listen to the statements and to complete the chart below.

	I heard this idea in the talk	I didn't hear this idea but can infer it from the information given	I did not hear this idea in the talk and cannot infer it from the information given
11.			
12.			
13.			
14.			

2. Using and Expanding on the Information in the Talk

a. Recapping the Information From Your Notes. Use your notes to recap the information you learned about African and Asian elephants. Present the information to the class or to one of your classmates.

b. Expanding on the Information in the Talk. Discuss the following questions with a classmate:

1. What are the most important working animals in your country? What kind of temperament do they have? Are they treated well?

2. Have you ever been to the circus? What were some of the animals you saw? What kinds of things were these animals trained to do? Is it ethical to use animals in circuses for entertainment?

3. Do you think it's good for people to have animals as pets? If so, what kinds of animals make good pets? Have you ever had a pet? What was it? What was its name?

4. Many animals such as the elephant, the giant panda, and the koala bear are endangered species, that is, they are close to extinction. Do you feel human beings have a responsibility to try to save these animals from extinction? Why or why not?

5. Do animals have rights equal to humans? Why or why not?

B. The Listening Expansion

TASK 1.

Completing a Sketch

I am going to talk about my two sisters, Alice and Betty. Alice and Betty are very different from each other. Look at the pictures of Alice and Betty in your workbook. As you can see, these sketches are incomplete. I will describe my sisters in detail and you will complete the sketches from my description. For example, I will say, "My two sisters have different hair styles. Alice has short, curly hair while Betty has long, straight hair." Now take your pencil or pen and draw short, curly hair on Alice and long, straight hair on Betty. Don't worry about how well you draw. Just do your best and have fun completing the sketches.

How did you do? Were you able to get all the details? Did you complete the sketches? Listen again as I describe my sisters. This will give you a chance to fill in any details you missed the first time.

After you have listened to the story for the second time, compare your sketches with another student's sketch in class or with the sketches in the back of the book.

TASK 2.

Listening Dictation

I'd like to tell you about my two brothers, Charles and David. Look at the pictures. Charles and David are a lot alike. They have many similarities. I am going to tell you some things that are very similar about Charles and David. I want you to write exactly what I say. This is a dictation. Be careful with the spelling and punctuation. Use your pictures to help you. Remember to write exactly what I say. Are you ready?

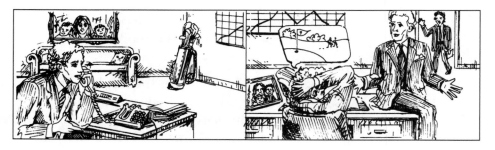

1. _____

2. _____

3. _____

4. _____

LISTENING FACTOID ▶ Listen to a talk about a young elephant who appeared to think he was a buffalo.

CHAPTER 2

LINCOLN AND KENNEDY

Similar Destinies

I. The Prelistening Task

A. Listening Preparation

Two of the most famous presidents in American history were Abraham Lincoln and John F. Kennedy. Do you know when each of these men was President of the United States? Do you know what was happening in the country while they were in office? Do you know how each man died?

You will learn the answers to these questions and some interesting facts about Kennedy and Lincoln. Although they lived in different centuries and were different in many ways, you will learn that there were some interesting similarities in the personal and political lives of these two men.

B. Preview of Vocabulary and Sentences

background the total experience, training, and education of a person; a person's history

- John F. Kennedy and Abraham Lincoln had very different family and educational *backgrounds.*

century a period of 100 years; 1801–1900, for example

- Kennedy lived in the 20th *century*; Lincoln lived in the 19th *century.*

formal schooling education acquired in school

- Lincoln had only one year of *formal schooling.*

coincidences two events that occur at the same time by accident but seem to have some connection; accidentally similar occurrences

- Books have been written about the strange *coincidences* in the lives of Lincoln and Kennedy.

Congressman/Congresswoman a man or woman who is a member of Congress, the lawmaking branch of the U.S. government

- Both Lincoln and Kennedy began their political careers as U.S. *Congressmen.*

U.S. House of Representatives; the House; Congress one of the lawmaking branches of the U.S. government

- Lincoln was elected to the *U.S. House of Representatives* in 1847 while Kennedy was elected to the *House* in 1947. They went to *Congress* just 100 years apart.

civil unrest demonstrations and protests by people against the government

- Both Kennedy and Lincoln were President during years of *civil unrest* in the United States.

civil rights demonstrations marches and meetings to protest unfair treatment of black people and other minorities

- During Kennedy's term in office, civil unrest took the form of *civil rights demonstrations.*

the American Civil War the war within the United States between the North and the South from 1861 to 1865

to assassinate to murder an important person in a planned, surprise attack
- Kennedy and Lincoln were both *assassinated* while in office.

destiny the course of happenings or events believed to be arranged by a superhuman power or powers, the fate of a person
- There are similarities in the *destinies* of Kennedy and Lincoln.

impact a powerful effect
- Kennedy and Lincoln had a tremendous *impact* on the social and political life in the United States.

C. Rhetorical Listening Cues

In this talk the speaker compares and contrasts John F. Kennedy and Abraham Lincoln. The speaker first talks about the differences between the two men and then discusses their similarities. The speaker uses words and phrases which signal differences, words such as "but," "on the other hand," "while," "whereas," and "different." The speaker also uses words to signal similarities between the two presidents, words such as "both," and "neither," "similarly," "also," and "furthermore."

II. The Main Listening Task

A. Initial Listening

Now let's listen to a talk about the similarities and differences between Kennedy and Lincoln. It may help you to concentrate on the talk if you close your eyes while listening. Just relax and listen carefully.

B. Mental Rehearsal and Review of the Talk

Let's listen to the talk once again. This time the talk will be given in message units. Please repeat each unit to yourself *silently* after you hear it. Remember, don't say the units out loud.

C. Consolidation

You will now hear the entire talk once again. While listening, take notes on the information contained in the talk.

III. The Postlistening Task

A. The Comprehension Check

1. Recognizing Information and Checking Accuracy

Answer the questions you hear by writing down short answers in the space provided. It is not necessary to write a complete sentence to answer each question.

1. _____

2. _____

3. _____

4. _____

5. _____

6. _____

7. _____

8. _____

9. _____

CHECK YOUR ANSWERS

10. _____

2. Using and Expanding on the Information in the Talk

a. Recapping the Information From Your Notes. Use your notes to recap the information you learned about the lives and careers of Lincoln and Kennedy. Present the information to the class or to one of your classmates.

b. Expanding on the Information in the Talk. Discuss with a classmate the following questions and issues.

1. Abraham Lincoln provided us with many memorable quotations. Read the quotation listed below and explain (1) what it means to you, and (2) what the quote says about how people do (or should) treat one another:

   As a nation, we began by declaring that "all men are created equal." We now practically read it "All men are created equal, except Negroes." When the Know-Nothings get control, it will read, "all men are created equal, except Negroes, and foreigners, and

Catholics." When it comes to this, I should prefer emigrating to some other country where they make no pretense of loving liberty . . . . (Abraham Lincoln, 1855)

2. After the death of his son Willie, Lincoln was persuaded by his wife to participate in several séances held in the White House. The President was deeply interested in psychic phenomena and wanted to communicate with his dead son. Once Lincoln reported that he had attended a séance in which a piano was raised and moved around the room. It was the professional opinion of the mediums who had worked with him that Lincoln was definitely the possessor of extraordinary psychic powers.

   Answer the following questions in discussion with a classmate:
   (a) Do you believe some people have psychic powers?
   (b) Would you attend a séance if you had the opportunity to do so? If yes, why? If no, why not?
   (c) Do you believe the dead can make contact with the living?
   (d) Do you believe in an afterlife? If not, why not? If so, what is the afterlife going to be like?
   (e) Do you believe in reincarnation? Why or why not?

3. There have been many conflicting views of who killed John Kennedy. Do you believe that Lee Harvey Oswald, acting alone, assassinated Kennedy? Explain why you believe in the "lone assassin" theory or the "conspiracy" theory.

4. Which of the following positions would you defend?

   Assassination of a head of state is never justified.

   Assassination of a head of state may, under certain circumstances, be justified.

5. John Kennedy provided us with many memorable quotations. Read the quotation listed below and explain (1) what it means to you, and (2) what the quote says about homelessness in America or any country.

   "If a free society cannot help the many who are poor, it cannot save the few who are rich." (Inaugural address, 1961)

6. What does the following story say about how people "rally around" (or support) their leaders during times of crisis?

   According to the polls, Kennedy's highest rating as President came right after the invasion of Cuba at the Bay of Pigs, as the American people rallied to support their President in difficult times, and 82% expressed approval of his handling of the job. No one was more amazed at this development than Kennedy. "My God," he said . . . . "The worse I do the more popular I get."

   Former U.S. President George Bush also experienced high levels of popular support after the Gulf War only to be defeated in the election two years later. Is it natural for people to rally around political figures when fighting wars? Should people be careful about doing this?

B. The Listening Expansion

TASK 1.

A Dictation of Similarities

The wives of the two Presidents were first ladies Jacqueline Kennedy and Mary Todd Lincoln. There were some similarities between the two women. You will hear five statements about the two women. Listen and write down exactly what you hear about Mrs. Kennedy and Mrs. Lincoln.

Mrs. Lincoln

Mrs. Kennedy

1. _____

2. _____

3. _____

4. _____

CHECK YOUR ANSWERS

5. _____

TASK 2.

Detecting Similarities and Differences

Another interesting similarity between Kennedy and Lincoln was the fact that both Presidents had vice-presidents named Johnson. Lincoln's vice-president was named Andrew Johnson. Kennedy's vice-president was named Lyndon Johnson. These two vice-presidents shared some similarities and had some differences between them. Listen to five statements about the two men. If the statement tells how the men were similar, circle the word "SIMILARITY." If the statement tells us they were different, circle the word "DIFFERENCE."

Andrew Johnson

Lyndon Johnson

1.   SIMILARITY   DIFFERENCE

2.   SIMILARITY   DIFFERENCE

3.   SIMILARITY   DIFFERENCE

4.   SIMILARITY   DIFFERENCE

CHECK YOUR ANSWERS

5.   SIMILARITY   DIFFERENCE

LISTENING FACTOID ▶ Abraham Lincoln is known as "The Great Emancipator" because he freed the slaves in the United States, but did he really? And does he deserve the title "The Great Emancipator"? Listen.

CHAPTER 3

THE *TITANIC* AND THE *ANDREA DORIA*

Tragedies at Sea

I. The Prelistening Task

A. Listening Preparation

People have been traveling by boat or ship for 3,000 years or more. During this time, many people have lost their lives in boating accidents or shipwrecks. Two of the most famous shipwrecks occurred in the 20th century. One wreck occurred in the early 1900s, and one occurred in the mid 1900s.

The names of the ships that went down at sea were the *Titanic* and the *Andrea Doria*. Almost everybody has heard of the *Titanic*. There was a movie made about the sinking of the *Titanic*. Did you see the movie? The shipwreck of the *Andrea Doria* is perhaps not as well known even though this shipwreck occurred only about 30 years ago. At the time of the sinking of the *Andrea Doria*, many news reporters compared the sinking of the *Andrea Doria* with the sinking of the *Titanic*. There *were* some similarities, but there were even more differences between these two tragic shipwrecks. In this talk you will learn about both the similarities and the differences between the sinking of the *Titanic* and the sinking of the *Andrea Doria*.

B. Preview of Vocabulary and Sentences

luxury liner a ship that provides passengers with beautiful, comfortable rooms to sleep in, games to play, and excellent food to eat. It costs a lot of money to travel on such a ship.

- On the morning of April 10, 1912, the *luxury liner* the *Titanic* left England on a voyage to New York.

to shock to surprise greatly; to astonish

- The sinking of these two huge ships *shocked the world.*

tragedy a very sad or terrible event; a mishap; a disaster

- Reports of these two *tragedies* filled the newspapers for days.

heroism great courage and bravery; valor; boldness

villainy corrupt, evil, and cowardly conduct

- As each ship was sinking, there were acts of *heroism* and acts of *villainy*.

coward a person who will not face danger bravely; a person who does not demonstrate courage in the face of fear or danger

- There were some people who acted like *cowards.*

disaster an event that happens suddenly and that causes great damage or suffering; a catastrophe

- There are differences between these great ship *disasters.*

iceberg a large mass of ice that has broken away from a glacier and that is floating in the ocean

- The *Titanic* struck an *iceberg.*

to collide with to crash into; to smash into

- The *Andrea Doria collided with* another ship.

lookout a person on a ship who watches for unexpected danger to the ship, such as an iceberg

- The *lookout* was able to see the iceberg only moments before the ship struck it.

to survive to remain alive after a dangerous situation; to live through a life-threatening event

- Over 700 people *survived* the sinking of the *Titanic.*

to rescue to save from danger or death

- There were about half the number of lifeboats needed to *rescue* all the people aboard the ship.

crew those who operate and run a ship

- The passengers and *crew* of the *Andrea Doria* were very lucky.

C. Rhetorical Listening Cues

In this talk the speaker discusses the similarities and differences between the sinking of two great ocean liners. The similarities are discussed first. The speaker uses words or phrases that indicate similarity, such as "both," "also," and "another similarity." The speaker also shows similarity by giving certain information about the *Titanic* and then by giving similar information about the *Andrea Doria.* For example, the speaker talks about when the *Titanic* left England and what happened to her four days later. And then the speaker tells when the *Andrea Doria* left Italy and what happened to her eight days later.

The speaker also uses certain words and phrases to signal the differences between the two ship accidents. The speaker uses expressions such as "while," "another contrast was . . . ," "but," and "however." As with the similarities, the speaker shows differences by giving certain information about one of the ships, and then by immediately giving contrasting information about the other ship. For example, the speaker mentions how many people died on the *Titanic* and then tells how many died on the *Andrea Doria*. The numbers of deaths for the two ships were very different.

II. The Main Listening Task

A. Initial Listening

Now let's listen to a talk about the similarities and differences between the sinking of two great ocean liners, the *Titanic* and the *Andrea Doria*. If you wish, close your eyes while listening. Just relax and listen carefully.

B. Mental Rehearsal and Review of the Talk

All right. Let's listen to the talk once again. This time, the talk will be given in message units. Please repeat each unit to yourself *silently* after you hear it. Remember, don't say the units out loud.

C. Consolidation

You will now hear the whole talk once again. As you listen, take notes on the information contained in the talk.

III. The Postlistening Task

A. The Comprehension Check

1. Recognizing Information and Checking Accuracy

For questions 1–5 you will hear multiple choice questions about the information presented in the talk. Listen to each question and decide whether (a), (b), (c), or (d) is the best answer to the question.

_____ **1.** (a) Italy
 (b) England
 (c) New York
 (d) none of the above

_____ **2.** (a) They were both luxury liners.
 (b) They were both crossing the Atlantic when they sank.
 (c) People believed that both ships were unsinkable.
 (d) all of the above

_____ **3.** (a) The *Andrea Doria* sank, but the *Titanic* did not.
 (b) The *Andrea Doria* carried enough lifeboats for the people on the ship, but the *Titanic* did not.
 (c) The *Titanic* had radar; however, the *Andrea Doria* did not.
 (d) The *Andrea Doria* carried passengers, but the *Titanic* did not.

_____ **4.** an act of _____
  (a) bravery
  (b) heroism
  (c) villainy
  (d) all of the above

_____ **5.** (a) More people died on
     the *Andrea Doria.*
  (b) Fewer people died on
     the *Andrea Doria.*
  (c) About the same
     number of people died
     on both ships.
  (d) none of the above

For questions 6–11, you will hear six statements about ideas. If the speaker mentioned the idea in the talk, put a check in the box "*I heard this idea in the talk.*" If, however, the idea was not mentioned in the talk, but you could infer the idea from the information given in the talk, put a check in the box, "*I didn't hear this idea but can infer it from the information given.*" Finally, if the idea you hear was not mentioned, and could not be inferred from the talk, check the box "*I did not hear this idea in the talk and cannot infer it from the information given.*"

	I heard this idea in the talk	I didn't hear this idea but can infer it from the information given	I did not hear this idea in the talk and cannot infer it from the information given
6.			
7.			
8.			
9.			
10.			
11.			

Now, you create four statements about the talk yourself. Ask a classmate to listen to the statements and to complete the chart below.

	I heard this idea in the talk	I didn't hear this idea but can infer it from the information given	I did not hear this idea in the talk and cannot infer it from the information given
12.			
13.			
14.			
15.			

2. Using and Expanding on the Information in the Talk

a. Recapping the Information From Your Notes.   Use your notes to recap the information you learned about the sinking of the *Titanic* and the *Andrea Doria*. Present the information to the class or to one of your classmates.

b. Expanding on the Information in the Talk.   Discuss the following questions with a classmate:

1. The expression "Women and children first!" means that all women and children should be rescued from danger before any men are saved. Do you agree with this? Why or why not?

2. It is traditional that anyone who finds a shipwreck like the *Titanic* can salvage all the valuables such as gold, silver, and money. However, even though the remains of the *Titanic* have been found, many people feel very strongly that the *Titanic* should be left undisturbed. Do you agree? Why or why not?

3. Do you agree with this statement?—During terrible disasters like shipwrecks, fires, and earthquakes, most people think only of saving themselves.

B. The Listening Expansion

TASK 1.   **A Dramatization of Senator Smith Questioning a Survivor**

Listen to and read the following story which will help you to understand the conversations which will follow between Senator Smith and Officer Pitman, a crewman and survivor of the *Titanic*.

There were many terrible questions that were asked after the *Titanic* went down at sea. For example, why had the ship been called "unsinkable" when it actually sank within $2\frac{1}{2}$ hours after it struck the iceberg? Why had the captain of the ship ignored warnings about icebergs? Why did the *Titanic* have only enough lifeboats on it for about half the number of people on the ship? Why were about one third of the people who survived the shipwreck members of the crew?

But perhaps the most terrible question of all was this: Why were some of the lifeboats in the water after the *Titanic* sank *half empty?* The lifeboats in the water had enough room for more than 1,100 people, but only about 700 people were saved. Nearly 1,000 people were left freezing in the water after the ship went down. Many lifeboats were only a few hundred yards away from the people in the water, but those in the lifeboats refused to return and try to save any of the people still in the water. One man who had been floating in the freezing water before he was finally able to climb into one of the lifeboats later said this: "The partially filled lifeboats standing by, only a few hundred yards away, never came back. Why on earth they did not come back is a mystery. How could any human being fail to heed those cries?"

Only a few days after the *Titanic* sank, the U.S. Senate began an official American investigation to answer this question and other questions. The Senate investigation was headed by Senator William Smith. One of the many survivors Senator Smith questioned was Third Officer Herbert J. Pitman. Officer Pitman had been in charge of one of the lifeboats. After the *Titanic* sank, Officer Pitman tied his lifeboat to another lifeboat. There was room for 60 more people from the *Titanic* in these two boats. Listen now as Senator Smith questions Officer Pitman. Listen as Officer Pitman tries to explain why he did not return to pick up the people who were floating around in the freezing water and who were crying for help after the *Titanic* disappeared under the water. Senator Smith begins:

TASK 2.

Deciding Whether You Agree or Disagree With Stated Opinions

Listen to the following statements about what you just heard between Senator Smith and Officer Pitman. If you agree, circle AGREE. If you disagree, circle DISAGREE.

1.   AGREE   DISAGREE

2.   AGREE   DISAGREE

3.   AGREE   DISAGREE

4.   AGREE   DISAGREE

5.   AGREE   DISAGREE

6.   AGREE   DISAGREE

7.   AGREE   DISAGREE

8.   AGREE   DISAGREE

9.   AGREE   DISAGREE

10. AGREE   DISAGREE

CHECK YOUR ANSWERS

11. AGREE   DISAGREE

Now explain to your instructor or a classmate why you agree or disagree with these opinions. (Replay the tape or consult the tapescript if necessary.)

UNIT FIVE

FOCUS ON
Causal Analysis

Causal analysis is a way of analyzing the reasons responsible for a certain result. It is often used by speakers or writers in presenting an explanation or argument. The reasons are usually presented in a certain order, either from most to least important or from least to most important.

CHAPTER 1

THE AMERICAN CIVIL WAR

Why It Happened

I. The Prelistening Task

A. Listening Preparation

In most wars two or more countries fight against each other; however, in a civil war the citizens within one country fight against one another. All wars are terrible, but civil wars are especially terrible because brothers sometimes fight against one another and sometimes kill one another. Like most wars, civil wars are usually caused by disagreements over religion, politics, or economics. In other words, they are fought because of (1) different religious beliefs, (2) political differences, or (3) differences between social or economic systems.

In this talk you will learn about the two main causes of the American Civil War. This war resulted from basic social and economic differences between the northern and southern parts of the United States. The two main issues dividing the North and the South of the country were (1) slavery, and (2) the preservation of the United States as one country.

B. Preview of Vocabulary and Sentences

friction a continuous disagreement over ideas or opinions; a clashing between two persons or groups of opposed views
- One of the causes of the war was the *friction* between the North and the South over the issue of slavery.

foundation a base or support which holds something up; understructure
- Slavery was the *foundation* of the entire economy and way of life in the South.

plantation a large southern estate or farm on which crops such as cotton and tobacco were grown, formerly by black slaves
- In the South there were many large cotton *plantations* which used hundreds of black slaves.

attitude a way of thinking, acting, or feeling; a point of view
- The northern *attitude* against slavery made the Southerners angry.

conflict a long fight or struggle; a war; a clash
- There were other causes of the *conflict* between the North and the South.

domination control; supremacy; mastery
- Many Southerners began to fear northern *domination.*

the Union the United States as it existed between 1776 and 1861; the northern side in the Civil War
- Many Southerners believed that the South should leave *the Union.*

the Confederate States of America the group of 11 southern states that seceded from the United States in 1860–1861
- They called the new country *the Confederate States of America.*

to secede to withdraw from a political alliance or organization
- The southern states decided to *secede* from the Union.

to preserve to keep together; to maintain

- The Civil War *preserved* the United States as one country.

C. Rhetorical Listening Cues

In this talk the speaker explains two of the most important causes of the American Civil War. The speaker uses certain words and phrases to signal the *reasons* or *causes* of the conflict, words and phrases such as: "The main reason . . . ," "Because . . . ," "Because of . . . ," "One of the important causes . . . ," "Other causes were . . . ," "Since . . . ."

The speaker also uses certain words and phrases to introduce *results* or *effects*, such as: "As a result . . . ," "Consequently . . . ," " . . . so . . . that . . . ," " . . . resulted in . . . ," " . . . caused . . . ," " . . . led to . . . ."

II. The Main Listening Task

A. Initial Listening

Now let's listen to a talk about the causes and effects of the American Civil War. It may help you to concentrate on the talk if you close your eyes while you listen. Just relax and listen carefully.

B. Mental Rehearsal and Review of the Talk

Let's listen to the talk once again. This time, the talk will be given in message units. Please repeat each unit to yourself *silently* after you hear it. Remember, don't say the units out loud.

C. Consolidation

You will now hear the whole talk once again. As you listen to the talk, take notes on the information you hear.

III. The Postlistening Task

A. The Comprehension Check

1. Recognizing Information and Checking Accuracy

For questions 1–10 you will hear multiple choice questions about the information presented in the talk. Listen to each question and decide whether (a), (b), (c), or (d) is the best answer to the question asked.

_____ 1. (a) over 100 years
  (b) for 4 years
  (c) in 1865
  (d) in 1861

_____ 2. the issue of _____
  (a) religion
  (b) slavery
  (c) history
  (d) crime

___ 3. The South's economy was ___.
  (a) based on cotton and tobacco
  (b) dependent on slave labor
  (c) both a and b
  (d) neither a nor b

___ 4. The North ___.
  (a) had smaller farms
  (b) grew a variety of crops
  (c) did not use slave labor
  (d) all of the above

___ 5. The growth of industry in the North ___.
  (a) increased the use of slave labor
  (b) resulted in increased population and money
  (c) increased southern domination of the North
  (d) increased the production of cotton and tobacco

___ 6. (a) The North abolished slavery.
  (b) Abraham Lincoln was elected President.
  (c) The slaves tried to secede and form their own country.
  (d) The South did not want to become industrialized like the North.

___ 7. (a) the Southern States of America
  (b) the Slave States of America
  (c) the Cotton States of America
  (d) the Confederate States of America

___ 8. The North went to war in order to ___.
  (a) abolish slavery
  (b) keep the United States one country
  (c) get control over the cotton plantations
  (d) force the South to become industrialized

___ 9. (a) The slaves helped the North.
  (b) The Southerners did not fight very hard.
  (c) The South depended on slaves to fight for them.
  (d) The North had greater industrial power and wealth.

___ 10. (a) It industrialized the South very quickly.
  (b) The South realized that slavery was evil.
  (c) It abolished slavery in the United States.
  (d) none of the above

You will hear 10 statements about the American Civil War. If the statement is true, put a T on the line next to the number of the statement. If the statement you hear is false, put an F on the line. If the truth cannot be determined *from the information given in the talk,* put a ? on the line.

11. ___   12. ___   13. ___   14. ___   15. ___

CHECK YOUR ANSWERS

16. ___   17. ___   18. ___   19. ___   20. ___

2. Using and Expanding on the Information in the Talk

a. Recapping the Information From Your Notes. Use your notes to recap the information you learned about the American Civil War. Present the information to the class or to one of your classmates.

b. Expanding on the Information in the Talk. Discuss with a classmate the following issues concerning the conduct of war:

1. Martin Luther King said, "We must learn to live together as brothers or perish together as fools." When will people learn to live together as brothers and sisters in a community of brotherhood and sisterhood? Will any event in the future make them forget about conducting war against one another? Do you think it is possible for all people to live together as brothers and sisters? Why or why not? If it is not possible, do you agree that we will all perish together? Why or why not?

2. It is said that "Older men declare war, but it is youth who must fight and die." Do you think this is true? If so, is it fair? Explain.

3. In his 1961 Inaugural speech, John Kennedy said, "Let us never negotiate out of fear. But let us never fear to negotiate." What is the most effective way to negotiate peace in the troubled regions of the world? Do you know of any situations in the world where JFK's advice would be useful?

4. Abraham Lincoln once said, "A house divided against itself cannot stand." What does this mean? Does this saying have any application to today's world?

B. The Listening Expansion

TASK 1.

A Listening Dictation

Listen as each sentence is spoken one time. Then write the sentence as it is dictated for the second time. After all sentences have been dictated, they will be repeated for a third time. Check that you have written down each and every word you hear. Notice the expressions that signal "cause and effect" relationships, such as (1) *because,* (2) *since,* (3) *as a result of,* (4) *because of,* and (5) *due to the fact that.*

1. _____

2. _____

3. _____

4. _____

CHECK YOUR ANSWERS

5. _____

TASK 2.

Guessing Possible Causes of Events

Listen to the following situations and then give some possible causes for the events described in the situations. For example, listen to the following situation:

A man and woman are sitting at a table in a restaurant. They have just finished dinner. Both the man and the woman look worried about something. The man has his wallet out on the table. He is showing it to the woman. He looks upset. What might be the cause of his upset?

1.

There could be many possible reasons for the man's upset. One of them might be that he forgot to put his money into his wallet when he left the house. Maybe he forgot to cash his paycheck after work and he doesn't have any money as a result. Perhaps the woman asked him for a loan of some money, and he is showing her that he doesn't have much money. What do you think? You may write your answers on a piece of paper or tell one of your classmates or your teacher your ideas.

2.

Possible causes: _____

3.

Possible causes: _____

4.

Possible causes: _____

5.

Possible causes: _____

6.

Possible causes: _____

 LISTENING FACTOID A book was partially responsible for the start of the great American Civil War. What was it? Listen.

CHAPTER 2

DINOSAURS
Why They Disappeared

I. The Prelistening Task

A. Listening Preparation

The word "dinosaur" means terrible lizard. About 150 million years ago, dinosaurs roamed the earth. There were many kinds of dinosaurs. Some of the dinosaurs were as small as chickens, while other dinosaurs were as large as houses. Dinosaurs were very successful animals on the earth for millions of years, but there are no dinosaurs on the earth today. Dinosaurs are extinct. They have been extinct for 65 million years. What happened to these animals that had lived so successfully on the earth for so many millions of years? Why did they become extinct? No one can be absolutely sure, of course. Many theories have been proposed since scientists began to take an interest in the fate of these incredible creatures.

In this talk you will hear about two current theories explaining why the dinosaurs disappeared from the earth. The theories are (1) the climatic change theory; and (2) the asteroid or comet theory. Listen as these two theories are explained to you.

B. Preview of Vocabulary and Sentences

to propose a theory to suggest an explanation for why something happens; an explanation based on observation and reasoning

- Several *theories* have been *proposed* about why the dinosaurs disappeared from the face of the earth.

to become extinct to have disappeared from the face of the earth

- Climatic changes caused the dinosaurs *to become extinct.*

severe very serious; grave

- The cold weather finally resulted in a *severe* shortage of food for the dinosaurs.

to dwindle to decrease in amount; to lessen

- The dinosaurs disappeared gradually as the earth became colder and as their food supply *dwindled.*

evidence an outward sign of the truth or falsehood of something

- Today there is new *evidence* that the dinosaurs did not disappear gradually, but that they disappeared quickly and suddenly.

asteroid one of the thousands of small planetlike bodies that revolve around the sun

- This theory is known as the *asteroid* theory.

comet a heavenly body made up of ice, frozen gases, and dust particles. It has a bright head and a long tail of light.

- The asteroid theory states that a huge asteroid, or perhaps a *comet*, hit the earth about 65 million years ago.

to block out the sun to prevent the light of the sun from reaching the surface of the earth

- The huge dust cloud covered the whole earth and *blocked out the sun* for months.

rare earth element one of the uncommon substances, such as plutonium, that is composed of atoms that are all chemically alike

- Scientists recently found large amounts of the *rare earth element* called iridium all over the world.

layer of the earth one thickness of the earth

- Iridium was found in *layers of the earth* that are 65 million years old.

to speculate to make a guess based on an observation and some evidence

- Scientists *speculate* that this iridium was brought to earth 65 million years ago when a comet or asteroid hit the earth.

to debate to give reasons for and against; to argue formally for or against

- Today scientists *debate* the two theories: the climatic change theory and the asteroid theory.

lizard a reptile with four legs, a long tail, and a scaly body

- In the future new evidence may be found that supports a totally new theory of why the terrible *lizards* died out.

C. Rhetorical Listening Cues

In this talk the speaker discusses two possible causes of the dinosaurs' disappearance from the earth. The speaker will use some words and phrases which signal causes and/or effects. The speaker will use words and phrases such as "was caused by," "since," "why," "caused," and "resulted in."

II. The Main Listening Task

A. Initial Listening

Now let's listen to a talk about the extinction of the dinosaurs. It may help you to concentrate on the talk if you close your eyes while you listen. Just relax and listen carefully.

B. Mental Rehearsal and Review of the Talk

Let's listen to the talk once again. This time, the talk will be given in message units. Please repeat each unit to yourself *silently* after you hear it. Remember, don't say the units out loud.

C. Consolidation

You will now hear the whole talk once again. As you listen to the talk, take notes on the information contained on the talk.

III. The Postlistening Task

A. The Comprehension Check

1. Recognizing Information and Checking Accuracy

For questions 1–4 you will hear multiple choice questions about the information presented in the talk. Listen to each question and decide whether (a), (b), (c), or (d) is the best answer to the question.

_____ 1. Dinosaurs _____.
   (a) were vegetarians
   (b) may disappear from the earth some day
   (c) were successful animals for millions of years
   (d) disappeared from the earth sometime in the past

_____ 2. The dinosaurs died out _____.
   (a) from breathing too much dust
   (b) from eating too much iridium
   (c) because an asteroid or a comet hit them
   (d) because their food supply was destroyed

_____ 3. (a) Dinosaurs disappeared quite suddenly.
   (b) Dinosaurs disappeared gradually and slowly.
   (c) A comet hit the earth 150 million years ago.
   (d) An asteroid or comet hit the earth 65 million years ago.

_____ 4. Both theories state that _____.
   (a) climatic change killed the dinosaurs
   (b) a food shortage caused dinosaurs to become extinct
   (c) an asteroid or a comet hit the earth 65 million years ago
   (d) there is no evidence which could explain why the dinosaurs disappeared

For questions 5–9, you will hear five statements about ideas. If the speaker mentioned the idea in the talk, put a check in the box *"I heard this idea in the talk."* If, however, the idea was not mentioned in the talk, but you could *infer* the idea from the information given in the talk, put a check in the box, *"I didn't hear this idea but can infer it from the information given."* Finally, if the idea you hear was not mentioned, and could not be inferred from the talk, check the box *"I did not hear this idea in the talk and cannot infer it from the information given."*

	I heard this idea in the talk	I didn't hear this idea but can infer it from the information given	I did not hear this idea in the talk and cannot infer it from the information given
5.			
6.			
7.			
8.			
9.			

CHECK YOUR ANSWERS

Now, you create four statements about the talk yourself. Ask a classmate to listen to the statements and to complete the chart below.

	I heard this idea in the talk	I didn't hear this idea but can infer it from the information given	I did not hear this idea in the talk and cannot infer it from the information given
10.			
11.			
12.			
13.			

2. Using and Expanding on the Information in the Talk

a. Recapping the Information From Your Notes. Use your notes to recap the information you learned about theories related to the extinction of dinosaurs. Present the information to the class or to one of your classmates.

b. Expanding on the Information in the Talk. Discuss with a classmate why you agree (or do not agree) with the following statements:

1. It's important for scientists to keep trying to figure out why dinosaurs disappeared.

2. We shouldn't worry so much about modern animals that are threatened with extinction since it's natural for animals to become extinct.

3. There is no danger today that an asteroid will hit the earth.

4. Human beings might become extinct someday.

B. The Listening Expansion

TASK 1.   **Recognizing Possible Causes of a Situation**

You will listen to a description of ten situations. After you listen to each situation described, read the four choices (a), (b), (c), and (d) and select the possible cause or causes of each situation.

For example, you will hear this situation described: "John has a broken leg." What are some possible causes of his broken leg? You will read in your book:

____ (a) John can't drive his car.

____ (b) John was in a car accident.

____ (c) John left work early today.

____ (d) John went skiing last weekend and fell.

John's leg might be broken because: (b) He was in a car accident. (That's possible.) Or (d) He went skiing last weekend and fell. (That's possible, too.) Choices (a) and (c) do not have anything to do with the possible *cause* of John's problem. Remember, find the possible cause or causes of a situation you hear described. Are you ready to begin?

1. ____ (a) The set is broken.

   ____ (b) The set isn't plugged in.

   ____ (c) The telephone is ringing.

   ____ (d) You forgot to pay your electricity bill.

2. ____ (a) The park is near her house.

   ____ (b) She doesn't feel very well.

   ____ (c) The weather is warm and sunny.

   ____ (d) She has to study for an exam.

3. ____ (a) The weather wasn't clear.

   ____ (b) The spaceship exploded on lift-off.

   ____ (c) One of the astronauts became sick.

   ____ (d) There was a problem with the computer on the spaceship.

4. ___ (a) He was often late to work.

  ___ (b) He found a new job immediately.

  ___ (c) He was sometimes rude to the customers.

  ___ (d) He doesn't have enough money now to pay his bills.

5. ___ (a) He grew up in Paris.

  ___ (b) He liked living in Paris.

  ___ (c) He went to Paris to get a job.

  ___ (d) His parents lived there in the 1940s.

6. ___ (a) The teacher didn't like Mary.

  ___ (b) Mary didn't study for the exam.

  ___ (c) The examination was too difficult for the class.

  ___ (d) Mary didn't understand the directions to the test.

7. ___ (a) Your doctor is out of town.

  ___ (b) You have dialed a wrong number.

  ___ (c) Nobody is in the doctor's office.

  ___ (d) The doctor's phone is out of order.

8. ___ (a) John was unlucky when he gambled.

  ___ (b) It's very expensive to fly to Monte Carlo.

  ___ (c) John doesn't have enough money to get home.

  ___ (d) John doesn't like to lose money when he gambles.

9. ___ (a) John didn't have a good job.

  ___ (b) John had married another woman.

  ___ (c) John was killed in a traffic accident.

  ___ (d) Mary realized that she didn't love John.

10. ___ (a) He is a soccer player.

  ___ (b) He is going to play tennis.

  ___ (c) He is getting ready to go jogging.

  ___ (d) He has just finished playing volleyball.

CHECK YOUR ANSWERS

TASK 2.

Predicting the Ending of a Story: Stating the Possible Results

You will listen to five stories. None of the stories has an ending. You will supply the ending. You will tell what happened in your own words. Tell the ending of each story to your teacher or to a classmate. Use your imagination to complete the story.

1. It's a cold and snowy night. (Listen.)

2. It's the last half of a championship soccer game. (Listen.)

3. A man is walking along the river. (Listen.)

4. You and your friend Bob are sitting in the movie theater waiting for the movie to begin. (Listen.)

5. You are waiting in line at the bank to cash a check. (Listen.)

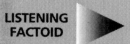
LISTENING FACTOID ▶ Listen to a talk about the unbelievable sizes of dinosaurs.

SCRIPTS
AND
ANSWER KEYS

II. The Main Listening Task

A. Initial Listening

Napoleon was a French soldier who became *emperor* of France. He was born in 1769 on the island of Corsica. When he was only ten years old, his father sent him to *military school* in France. Napoleon was not a very good student in most of his classes, but he *excelled* in mathematics and in military science. When he was sixteen years old, he joined the French army. In that year he began the military *career* that brought him *fame*, power, riches, and, finally, defeat. Napoleon became a general in the French army at the young age of twenty-four. Several years later he became emperor of the French Empire.

Napoleon was many things. He was, first of all, a brilliant military leader. His soldiers were ready to die for him. As a result, Napoleon won many, many military *victories*. At one time he *controlled* most of Europe, but many countries, including England, Russia, and Austria fought fiercely against Napoleon. His defeat—his end—came when he decided to attack Russia. In this military campaign against Russia, he *lost* most of his army.

The great French conqueror died alone—*deserted* by his family and his friends—in 1821. He died in 1821, alone and deserted. Napoleon was only fifty-one years old when he died.

B. Mental Rehearsal and Review of the Talk

Napoleon was a French soldier.
He became emperor of France.
He was born in 1769 in Corsica.
When he was ten, his father sent him to military school.
Napoleon was not a very good student.
He excelled in mathematics and in military science.
When he was sixteen, he joined the French army.
When he was sixteen, he began his military career.
His career brought him fame, power, riches, and, finally, defeat.
Napoleon became a general when he was twenty-four.
Several years later he became emperor.
Napoleon was a great military leader.
His soldiers were ready to die for him.
Napoleon won many military victories.
He controlled most of Europe.
Many countries fought against him.
Many countries, including England, Russia, and Austria, fought him.
His defeat came when he attacked Russia.
He lost most of his army.

Napoleon died alone in 1821.
He was deserted by his family and friends.
He was fifty-one years old when he died.

C. Consolidation

See II. A. (A version of II. A. is presented in the Consolidation.)

III. The Postlistening Task

A. The Comprehension Check

1. Recognizing Information and Checking Accuracy

1. When was Napoleon born? (a)

2. What kind of student was Napoleon in most of his classes? (d)

3. What did Napoleon's military career bring him? (d)

4. When did Napoleon become emperor of the French Empire? (d)

5. One reason that Napoleon won many military victories was that his soldiers were ready to fight to the death for him. (T)

6. Austria and Russia fought fiercely against Napoleon, but England did not. (F   England also fought against him.)

7. Many of Napoleon's family and friends were with him when he died. (F   He died alone and deserted by his family and friends.)

8. Napoleon died before he reached the age of fifty-two. (T)

B. The Listening Expansion

TASK 1.   **Completing a Map**

1. Moscow was the capital city of the Russian Empire during Napoleon's time. Find the Russian Empire on the map. Now write the word "Moscow" next to the star drawn on the Russian Empire. "Moscow" is spelled "M-o-s-c-o-w."

2. Good. Now find the city of Madrid on the map. Madrid was the capital of the Kingdom of Spain. Write the words "Kingdom of Spain" in the correct place on the map. "Kingdom" is spelled "K-i-n-g-d-o-m." "Spain" is spelled "S-p-a-i-n."

3. Another important capital city during Napoleon's age was Vienna. It was the capital of the Austrian Empire. Find Vienna on the map. Write the words "Austrian Empire" in the correct place on the map. That's "A-u-s-t-r-i-a-n" and "E-m-p-i-r-e."

4. North of the city of Vienna was the capital city of Berlin. Do you see Berlin on the map? Berlin was the major city of the Kingdom of Prussia. Fill in the word "P-r-u-s-s-i-a" in the correct place on the map. Spell Prussia correctly: "P-r-u-s-s-i-a."

5. And last, In Napoleon's time, between the Austrian Empire and the French Empire was the Confederation of the Rhine. Find the Confederation of the Rhine written on the map. Leipzig was its capital city. Write "Leipzig" on the map. Leipzig is spelled "L-e-i-p-z-i-g." Now the map is complete.

TASK 2.

Answering Questions About the Completed Map

1. Find the Kingdoms of Norway and Denmark on the map. What kingdom is east of Norway and Denmark? (the Kingdom of Sweden)

2. Which kingdom was located south of the Kingdom of Italy in Napoleon's day? (the Kingdom of Naples)

3. There was a small kingdom west of the Kingdom of Spain. What was the name of this small kingdom? (the Kingdom of Portugal)

4. In Napoleon's time, south of the Russian Empire lay the Ottoman Empire. Find the Ottoman Empire on the map. What was the capital city of this empire? Write it down. Be careful to spell it correctly. (Constantinople)

5. Find Finland on the map. Was Finland east or west of the Kingdom of Sweden? Write the word "east" or the word "west" in the correct space. (east)

6. The capital city of England was London. Was London north or south of the capital city of the French Empire? Write the correct word on the blank line. (north)

Listening Factoid

The cause of Napoleon's death at the age of 51 on the island of St. Helena is still a mystery. There is no doubt that he was a very sick man at the time of his death. One theory about the cause of his death is that he had stomach cancer. Another theory is that he was deliberately poisoned by a servant. A third theory also suggests that he was poisoned, but not by his servant. This third theory suggests that he was poisoned accidentally by fumes from the wallpaper in the house he lived in. A few years ago, samples of the wallpaper were analyzed and traces of arsenic were found in it. Arsenic is a powerful poison that was used in some of the dyes in wallpaper during the time that Napoleon lived. More than 170 years after his death, people are still speculating about the cause of his death.

II. The Main Listening Task

A. Initial Listening

Today many people who live in large metropolitan areas such as Paris and New York leave the city in the summer. They go to the mountains or to the seashore to escape the city noise and heat. Over 2,000 years ago, many rich Romans did the same thing. They left the city of Rome in the summer. Many of these wealthy Romans spent their summers in the city of Pompeii. Pompeii was a beautiful city; it was located on the ocean, on the *Bay of Naples.*

In the year *79 A.D.,* a young Roman boy who later became a very famous Roman historian was visiting his uncle in Pompeii. The boy's name was Pliny the Younger. One day Pliny was looking up at the sky. He saw a frightening *sight.* It was a very large dark cloud. This black cloud rose high into the sky. Rock and *ash* flew through the air. What Pliny saw was the *eruption*—the explosion—of the volcano, Vesuvius. The city of Pompeii was at the foot of Mt. Vesuvius.

When the volcano first erupted, many people were able to *flee* the city and to escape death. In fact, 18,000 people escaped the terrible disaster. Unfortunately, there was not enough time for everyone to escape. More than 2,000 people died. These unlucky people were *buried alive* under the volcanic ash. The eruption lasted for about three days. When the eruption was over, Pompeii was buried under 20 feet of volcanic rock and ash. The city of Pompeii was buried and forgotten for 1,700 years.

In the year 1748 an Italian farmer was *digging* on his farm. As he was digging, he uncovered a part of a wall of the ancient city of Pompeii. Soon *archaeologists* began to excavate—to dig—in the area. As time went by, much of the ancient city of Pompeii was uncovered. Today tourists come from all over the world to see the *ruins* of the famous city of Pompeii.

B. Mental Rehearsal and Review of the Talk

Two thousand years ago, many Romans left Rome in the summer.
Many of these wealthy Romans spent their summer in Pompeii.
Pompeii was located on the Bay of Naples.
In 79 A.D., a young Roman boy was visiting his uncle in Pompeii.
One day Pliny saw a frightening sight.
He saw a very large dark cloud.
This cloud rose high into the sky.
Pliny saw the eruption of Vesuvius.
Pompeii was at the foot of Vesuvius.
Many people were able to flee the city.
Eighteen thousand people escaped death.

More than 2,000 people died.
They were buried alive under the volcanic ash.
The eruption lasted for about three days.
Pompeii was buried under 20 feet of volcanic rock and ash.
Pompeii was forgotten for 1,700 years.
In 1748 an Italian farmer uncovered a part of Pompeii.
Archaeologists began to excavate in the area.
As time went by, much of the ancient city of Pompeii was uncovered.
Today tourists come from all over the world to see the ruins of Pompeii.

C. Consolidation

See II. A.

III. Postlistening Task

A. The Comprehension Check

1. Recognizing Information and Checking Accuracy

1. At what time of the year did wealthy Romans like to visit Pompeii? (in the summertime)

2. In what year did Pliny pay a visit to his uncle's house in Pompeii? (in 79 A.D.)

3. What did Pliny see when he was looking out over the Bay of Naples one day? (a large dark cloud)

4. Where was Pompeii located in relation to Mt. Vesuvius? (Pompeii was located at the foot of Mt. Vesuvius.)

5. When did an Italian farmer discover a part of an ancient wall of Pompeii? (in 1748)

6. Rome was located at the foot of Mt. Vesuvius. (F   Pompeii was located at the foot of Mt. Vesuvius.)

7. Most of the people of Pompeii were able to flee the city and to escape death. (T)

8. Pompeii was buried under two feet of volcanic ash. (F   Pompeii was buried under 20 feet of volcanic ash.)

9. Pompeii lay buried and forgotten between 79 A.D. and 1748. (T)

10. The Italian farmer was looking for the ancient city of Pompeii.
   (F   The farmer was digging on his farm.)

11. Tourists come to excavate the city of Pompeii. (F   Tourists come to see the ruins of the ancient city of Pompeii.)

B. The Listening Expansion

TASK 1.

Listening for Sequence Identification

Example 1:   John graduated from high school in the spring. He went to college in the fall.

These two sentences are in the correct time sequence. The event in the first sentence happened before the event in the second sentence. Write "yes" next to example 1.

Example 2:   He took the final examination on Friday. John studied very hard on Saturday for his final examination.

These sentences are not in the correct time sequence. Write "no" next to example 2.

1. Pliny went to Pompeii. The volcano erupted. (yes)

2. The city was covered with 20 feet of ash. A dark cloud rose high in the sky. (no)

3. A farmer discovered part of a buried wall. Archaeologists began to excavate the ancient city of Pompeii. (yes)

4. The volcano erupted in 79 A.D. Christ was born. (no)

5. A large dark cloud rose high in the sky. People fled from the city. (yes)

6. You learned how many people were killed at Pompeii. You heard the story of the city of Pompeii. (no)

TASK 2.

Listening to Complete and Use a Chart

The eruption of Mt. Vesuvius was probably the most famous eruption in history. However, the eruption of Mt. Vesuvius did not kill the most people of any volcanic eruption. Let's compare Mt. Vesuvius with some other famous volcanoes. In your book there is a chart with the names of six volcanoes. The chart tells you the name of the volcanic mountain, where it is located, the date of an eruption, and the approximate number of people who died in the eruption. Look at Mt. Vesuvius on the chart. This volcano is located in Italy. It erupted in 79 A.D. Approximately 2,000 people died in the eruption. Let's fill in the missing information—the information not on the chart—for the other volcanic mountains. Are you ready to write in the information and complete the chart? O.K. Let's begin with the next mountain on the chart—Cotopaxi. It is located in Ecuador. It erupted in 1877, and about 1,000 people died. Write the number 1,000 in the correct place. Now look at Krakatoa. It is located in Indonesia. It erupted in 1883 and killed about 36,000 people. Write the year 1883 in the correct place. Now lets complete the information for Mont Pelée, located in Martinique. It erupted in 1902, killing 38,000 people. Did you write 38,000 in the correct place? O.K. Next fill in the blank for Mount St. Helens in Washington State in the United States. It erupted in 1980 and 60 people were killed. Did you write 60 in the correct space? Finally, let's complete the chart for Mount Tambora in Indonesia. It erupted in 1815, killing 12,000 people. Twelve thousand people died in 1815. Now your chart should be complete.

Famous Volcanoes of the World			
Name	Location	Date of Eruption	Approximate Number of People Who Died
Vesuvius	Italy	79 A.D.	2,000
Cotopaxi	Ecuador	1877	(1,000)
Krakatoa	Indonesia	(1883)	36,000
Mont Pelée	Martinique	1902	(38,000)
Mount St. Helens	Washington State (U.S.A.)	1980	(60)
Mount Tambora	Indonesia	(1815)	(12,000)

1. Mt. Vesuvius (79 A.D.)
2. Mount Tambora (1815)
3. Cotopaxi (1877)
4. Krakatoa (1883)
5. Mont Pelée (1902)
6. Mount St. Helens (1980)

Listening Factoid

In 1951, an Australian pilot prevented his plane from being shot down—by flak from a volcano. The plane was flying over a volcano in Papua, New Guinea when the volcano suddenly erupted. It sent ash and flak 36,000 feet into the air. Bits of stone pounded against the plane's wings and fuselage, but the pilot kept control and flew the plane to safety. Incidentally, almost 3,000 people on the ground died as a result of the eruption of this volcano.

II. The Main Listening Task

A. Initial Listening

One of the most remarkable women in American history was Harriet Tubman. She was a woman of African descent who *was born in slavery* on a *Maryland plantation* in the year 1820. When she was only seven years old, she tried to run away from the plantation, but *she was captured* and severely beaten for trying to run away. In 1849, she escaped to Pennsylvania. Soon after her escape, she became a conductor on the Underground Railroad, which was not a real railroad. It was *an informal network of people* in the United States and Canada who believed slavery was wrong. They helped *runaway slaves* by *giving them shelter* on their journey out of the South. The members of the Underground Railroad helped hide the runaway or *fugitive slaves,* and then they "conducted" them to the next safe home or "station." After her escape from Maryland, Harriet Tubman returned to the South nineteen times to help other slaves escape north. Between 1850 and 1860, she helped more than 300 slaves escape to freedom in the North, including her own parents. She conducted many of these slaves along the Underground Railroad all the way to Canada.

In 1861, the American Civil War between the North and the South broke out, and Harriet went to help the army of the North, or, as it was also called, the Union Army. She worked as *a nurse* and helped to take care of thousands of recently freed slaves. Harriet Tubman served as a nurse for the North, but she also served as a *spy* and a *commando.* Let me tell you what this fearless woman did. In 1863, she and a Union officer led a band of 150 black soldiers on a raid against the army of the South, or, as it was called, the Confederate Army. Tubman and the soldiers destroyed a lot of army supplies and then led nearly 800 slaves out of the area to freedom.

When the war ended in 1865, Harriet was 45 years old, but her life was only about half over at that time. Between 1865 and 1913, Harriet continued her efforts to help others, particularly the poor, the sick and the homeless in the African-American community. She lived until 1913. When she died, she was 93 years old.

Harriet Tubman did not have an easy life, but she had a very remarkable life. She was *a small woman in stature,* but she was *a giant* in the story of the fight against slavery in the United States and, indeed, in the world.

B. Mental Rehearsal and Review of the Talk

One of the most remarkable women in American history was Harriet Tubman. She was a woman of African descent who was born in slavery on a Maryland plantation in 1820.

She tried to run away from the plantation.
She was captured and severely beaten.
In 1849, she escaped to Pennsylvania.
She became a conductor on the Underground Railroad.
The Underground Railroad was not a real railroad.
It was an informal network of people in the United States and Canada.
The people of the Underground Railroad believed slavery was wrong.
The people of the Underground Railroad helped hide the runaway (or fugitive) slaves.
They conducted the fugitive slaves to the next safe home or "station."
Tubman returned to the South nineteen times to help other slaves escape.
Between 1850 and 1860, she helped more than 300 slaves escape.
She helped her parents escape to freedom.
She conducted many of the slaves to Canada.
In 1861, The American Civil War broke out.
Harriet went to help the army of the North—the Union Army.
She worked as a nurse.
She also worked as a spy and a commando.
In 1863, she and a Union officer led 150 black soldiers on a raid against the army of the South—the Confederate Army.
They destroyed a lot of supplies and led nearly 800 slaves to freedom.
When the war ended in 1865, her life was only half over.
Between 1865 and 1913, she continued her efforts to help the poor, the sick and the homeless in the African-American community.
She lived until 1913.
She was 93 years old when she died.
She did not have an easy life.
She had a remarkable life.
She was a small woman in stature.
She was a giant in the fight against slavery in the United States and the world.

C. Consolidation

See II. A.

III. The Postlistening Task

A. The Comprehension Check

1. Recognizing Information and Checking Accuracy

1. What happened when young Harriet was returned to the plantation after she ran away? (a)

2. How many times did Harriet Tubman return to the South between 1850 and 1860 to lead slaves to the North? (a)

3. In what year did the American Civil War start? (c)

4. In what year did Harriet and a small band of soldiers carry out a raid against the Confederates? (b)

5. What do we call the soldiers who fought for the South during the American Civil War? (d)

6. She served as a scout for the Union Army during the Civil War. (HT)

7. This young officer in the Union army helped lead more than 800 slaves to freedom. (SH)

8. When she was 45 years old, she was elected leader of her country. (SH)

9. She was a nurse for the Confederate Army during the Civil War. (SH)

10. She had an easy life during her childhood. (SH)

B. The Listening Expansion

TASK 1.

Filling in Information and Answering Questions

The Struggle for Equal Civil Rights

At the beginning of the Civil War in 1861, there were more than four million African-Americans in the United States. About 89% of these people were enslaved in the South. When the Civil War ended in 1865, all the slaves were freed. The Congress of the United States in the next few years passed the 14th and 15th Amendments to the U.S. Constitution to guarantee these newly freed people equal civil rights, including the right to vote. However, Southern states almost immediately began to pass laws which segregated, or separated, black people in schools, public places, and housing. Both legal and illegal ways to prevent these people from voting were also used. Unfortunately, the U.S. Supreme Court in 1896 upheld a law in the Southern state of Louisiana which segregated black people on trains. The Supreme Court decided that "separate but equal" facilities were not against the Constitution. This decision led to about 50 years of institutionalized segregation in the South. Although segregation was never legal in the North, there was still widespread discrimination, and segregation in schools and housing was quite common. During World War II things began to change and by the end of the war, the military was completely desegregated. That is, segregation was ended in the military. During the 1940s and 1950s, more and more states began to pass laws against segregation and discrimination, and in 1954, the Supreme Court reversed its earlier "separate but equal" decision and decided that "separate but equal" facilities violated people's civil rights. The Supreme Court ordered that public schools be desegregated. In 1964 Congress passed the Civil Rights Act, which outlawed discrimination in public facilities, public education, labor unions, and employment. The Voting Rights Act, passed in 1965, helped to protect every person's right to vote. This brief outline of the struggle for equal civil rights emphasized the legal side of the struggle. The human side of the struggle is, of course, dramatic and moving, with great determination and courage shown by leaders and common people together.

From the information you have filled in, answer the following questions. Write short answers. Listen carefully to the question.

1. How many African-Americans were there in the United States when the Civil War began in 1861? (more than four million)

2. What percentage of these African-Americans were enslaved? (89%)

3. In what year did the U.S. Supreme Court decide that "separate but equal" facilities did *not* violate the U.S. Constitution? (1896)

4. In what year did the U.S. Supreme Court *reverse* the earlier "separate but equal" decision? (1954)

5. Is racial segregation legal anywhere in the United States today? (no)

TASK 2.

Reading to Put Sentences in Chronological Order

Martin Luther King, 1929–1968

Martin Luther King was born in the Deep South, in Atlanta, Georgia, in 1929, the son of a Baptist minister. He followed in his father's footsteps as a Baptist minister, but he also became the most influential leader of the civil rights movement of the 1950s and 1960s, organizing nonviolent protests against discrimination. One of the most important events that he was involved in began in December, 1955, when a black woman, Rosa Lee Parks, was arrested in Montgomery, Alabama. She was arrested for refusing to move to the back of the bus as the law required.

Following her arrest, Dr. King organized a successful black boycott of the buses. The success of the bus boycott showed how powerful the strategy of nonviolent resistance could be and increased his stature as a national leader for civil rights.

Probably the next most important historical event he was involved in was the March on Washington for Jobs and Freedom, where he gave his famous "I Have a Dream" speech in August of 1963. Congress passed the 1964 Civil Rights Act the next year. The same year that the Civil Rights Act was passed, Martin Luther King was awarded the Nobel Peace Prize. Although King had preached nonviolence as a way of life, he was assassinated in 1968, and his death sparked riots in more than 100 cities.

Answers:

1. H		6. F	
2. A		7. B	
3. G		8. D	
4. C		9. J	
5. E		10. I	

Listening Factoid

The mistreatment of African-Americans in the United States did not end when the Civil War ended. Harriet Tubman found this out at the hands of a white Northerner. Listen to this sad story. After the war, Tubman boarded a northbound train in Washington D.C. She was carrying a half-fare military pass because of her work for the Union Army during the war. She showed her pass to the white conductor on the train. He looked at the pass and told her that blacks were not permitted to travel at half-fare. With the help of three other men, the conductor dragged her out of the passenger car as the train's white passengers watched in silence. No one came to Tubman's aid as the four men threw her out of the passenger car into the baggage car. Her arm was hurt badly during the incident. Harriet Tubman, the only woman who had led troops in battle for the Union, had suffered injury from a civilian in the "free" North.

II. The Main Listening Task

A. Initial Listening

The first *power-driven flight of a plane* occurred in 1903 when Orville Wright flew his plane 120 feet at an airspeed of 30 miles per hour. He flew the plane 8 to 12 feet above the earth for 12 seconds. Just 26 years later, the first flight of a jet-powered plane was made. Today, jumbo jets can carry 500 people around the world, flying at speeds between 400 and 600 miles per hour. How does a plane weighing 85 *tons* ever get into the air? *Jet propulsion* puts the plane into the air. I can illustrate the principle of jet propulsion with a very simple demonstration that you can do yourself. I'll describe how you can make a rocket boat to illustrate the principle of jet propulsion and forward thrust.

To make a rocket boat, you need a few pieces of equipment. You need a *hollow* aluminum tube. The tube needs to have a lid or top that can *be twisted on and off*. (You can use a cigar tube for the experiment if you happen to know someone who smokes cigars!) You also need a hammer and nail, two pipe cleaners, some glue, some water, three small candles, and an aluminum tray. Ok. Listen carefully as I tell you how to make a rocket boat.

First, take the aluminum tube and *punch a hole in* its top or lid. Use the hammer and nail to punch this hole in the tube's lid. Next, fill the tube about half full with water. Put the lid on the tube and twist it closed. The next thing you need to do is to twist a pipe cleaner around each end of the tube. Then glue the tube and the pipe cleaners into an aluminum food tray. Take a look at the illustration to see how this should be done.

Now, put three small candles into the aluminum food tray underneath the tube. That's about it. You now have your rocket boat. Put the rocket boat into a pan or basin of water. After that, light the candles. In a few minutes, the rocket boat will move forward. The boat will be thrust forward by a *jet of exhaust steam* created when the water inside the tube is heated.

The next time you fly in a jet plane, think of this simple experiment and of all the amazing developments that have taken place in the design of plane and rocket engines since 1903.

B. Mental Rehearsal and Review of the Talk

The first power-driven flight of a plane occurred in 1903.
Orville Wright flew a distance of 120 feet at 30 miles per hour.
He flew 8 to 12 feet above the earth for 12 seconds.
Twenty-six years later, the first flight of a jet-powered plane occurred.
Jumbo jets can carry 500 people.

Jumbo jets fly between 400 and 600 miles per hour.
How does a plane weighing 85 tons get into the air?
Jet propulsion puts the plane into the air.
I'll describe how you can make a rocket boat.
You will need a hollow aluminum tube.
The tube needs a top or lid.
You need a hammer and nail, and two pipe cleaners.
You need water and glue.
You need three small candles and an aluminum food tray.
Punch a hole in the top of the tube.
Fill the tube about half full with water.
Twist a pipe cleaner around each end of the tube.
Glue the tube and the pipe cleaners into the tray.
Put three candles underneath the tube.
Put the rocket boat into a pan or basin of water.
Light the candles.
The rocket boat will move forward.
It will be thrust forward by a jet of exhaust steam.

C. Consolidation

See II. A.

III. The Postlistening Task

A. The Comprehension Check

1. Recognizing Information and Checking Accuracy

1. How long did the first power-driven flight last? (a)

2. Where do you punch a hole with the hammer and nail? (a)

3. What holds the tube in the tray? (c)

4. What happens when the jet of exhaust steam escapes from the tube? (d)

5. To make the rocket boat, you need to use a hollow tube. (T)

6. The candles need to be small so that they fit beneath the hollow tube. (T)

7. The food tray should be made of a light-weight kind of metal. (T)

8. The water in the tube turns into steam when it is heated. (T)

B. The Listening Expansion

TASK 1. **Connecting the Processes**

(1) *First*, the target planet will be selected and (2) *after that*, it will be photographed and carefully mapped. The rocket carrying the spacecraft with the astronauts in it will be prepared for the voyage. (3) *In the meantime,* the men

and women astronauts will be selected and trained for the flight. When everything is ready, the rocket will blast off from earth. (4) *After some time,* The rocket will dock at an orbiting space station in order to refuel. (5) *After refueling* it will blast off from the space station and head toward the target planet. The trip will be long. (6) *After a long journey,* the spacecraft will enter the target planet's orbit. (7) *Next,* it will make a soft landing on the planet. (8) *Some time after that,* the astronauts will leave the spaceship and explore the planet. (9) *Finally,* they will reenter their mother ship and begin their preparation for the trip back to earth.

TASK 2.

Testing Your ESP

First get two sheets of paper with lines on them. You also need a deck of 52 playing cards. Next number the lines of both sheets of paper from 1 to 52. Then give one sheet of paper to your friend and keep the other one.

Now ask your friend to sit across the room from you where you cannot see the cards or what your friend is writing on his or her paper.

To begin the experiment, ask your friend to look at the top card and write the color of that card (red or black) next to number 1. Then ask him or her to send you the color of the card by visualizing the color in his or her mind. As soon as a color comes into your mind, write the color next to the number 1 on your paper. Your friend should continue this process until all 52 cards have been used. Do not check your answers until you both have gone through the whole deck of cards. Then check to see how many of your guesses were correct. By chance the average number of guesses should be 26 (1 out of 2). If you score 30 or more, you might have some powers of mental telepathy. Do the experiment several times to see whether you really might have some special psychic ability. Think of some ways you could use your psychic ability. Discuss your ideas with a friend, a classmate, or your teacher.

Listening Factoid

Just listen to this interesting fact about some expensive moon rocks.

The 12 Apollo astronauts who landed on the moon between 1969 and 1972 brought back to earth a total of 842 pounds of rocks and dust from the moon. Since the Apollo program cost the United States about $40 billion, the moon rocks and dust cost the U. S. about $3 million per ounce. They cost thousands of times their weight in gold.

II. The Main Listening Task

A. Initial Listening

Babies are able to communicate as soon as they are born without knowing how to speak any language at all. At first, they communicate by crying. This crying lets their parents know when they are hungry, or unhappy, or uncomfortable. However, they soon begin the process of acquiring their language. The first stage of language acquisition begins a few weeks after birth. At this stage, babies start to make *cooing noises* when they are happy. Then, around four months of age they begin to *babble*. Babies all over the world begin to babble around the same age, and they all begin to make the same kinds of babbling noises. By the time they are ten months old, however, the babbling of babies from different language backgrounds sounds different. For example, the babbling of a baby in a Chinese-speaking home sounds different from the babbling of a baby in an English-speaking home. Babies begin a new stage of language development when they begin to speak their first words. At first, they *invent* their own *words* for things. For example, a baby in an English-speaking home may say "baba" for the word "bottle" or "kiki" for "cat." In the next few months, babies will *acquire* a lot of words. These words are usually the names of things that are in the baby's environment, words for food or toys, for example. They will begin to use these words to communicate with others. For example, if a baby holds up an empty juice cup and says "juice," to his father, the baby seems to be saying, "I want more juice, Daddy" or "May I have more juice, Daddy?" This word "juice" is really a one-word sentence.

The next stage of language acquisition begins around the age of 18 months when the babies begin to say two-word sentences. They begin to use a kind of grammar to put these words together. The speech they produce is called *"telegraphic"* because the babies omit all but the most *essential* words. An English-speaking child might say something like "Daddy, up" which actually could mean "Daddy, pick me up, please." Between two and three years of age, young children begin to learn more and more grammar. For example, they begin to use the past tense of verbs. In other words, they begin to learn the rule for making the past tense of many verbs. The children begin to say things such as "I walked home" and "I kissed Mommy." They also begin to *overgeneralize* this new grammar rule and make a lot of grammar mistakes. For example, children often say such things as "I goed to bed" instead of "I went to bed," or "I eated ice cream" instead of "I ate ice cream." In other words, the children have learned the past tense rule for regular verbs such as "walk" and "kiss," but they haven't learned that they cannot use this rule for all verbs. Some verbs like "eat" are irregular, and the past tense forms for irregular verbs must be learned individually. Anyhow, these mistakes are normal, and the children will soon learn to use the past tense for regular and irregular verbs correctly. The children then continue to learn other grammatical structures in the same way.

If we stop to think about it, actually it's quite amazing how quickly babies and children all over the world learn their language and how similar the process is for babies all over the world.

B. Mental Rehearsal and Review of the Talk

Babies are able to communicate as soon as they are born.
At first, they communicate by crying.
This crying lets their parents know how they feel.
Their parents know if they are hungry, or unhappy, or uncomfortable.
Babies soon begin to acquire language.
The first stage begins a few weeks after birth.
They start to make cooing noises.
Around four months babies begin to babble.
All babies begin to babble at the same age.
They all make the same babbling noises.
By ten months the babbling of babies sounds different.
At this time a new stage of language learning begins.
Now babies begin to make their first words.
They invent their own words.
These words are the babies' own words for things, like "kiki" for cat.
Soon after, the babies begin to learn the names of many things.
These things are in their environment.
They learn the words for toys and food, for example.
They begin to use these words to communicate.
They begin to make one-word sentences.
For example, they hold up their cup and say "juice."
The next stage begins at about 18 months of age.
At 18 months they begin to make two-word sentences.
They use a kind of grammar to put these two words together.
This language is called "telegraphic" speech.
Telegraphic language has only the most essential words.
Between two and three years of age children learn more grammar rules.
For example, they begin to use the past tense rule for regular verbs.
They overgeneralize the past tense rule to irregular verbs.
They make lots of mistakes.
For example, they say "I goed sleep" instead of "I went to sleep."
Their mistakes are natural at this age.
They continue to learn more grammatical structures in the same way.
This process is similar for babies all over the world.

C. Consolidation

See II.A.

III. The Postlistening Task

A. The Comprehension Check

1. Recognizing Information and Checking Accuracy

1. At what age do babies begin to communicate? (a)

2. Which of the following is an example of "telegraphic" speech? (b)

3. At what age do children begin to use the past tense? (c)

4. At four months of age the babbling of babies sounds the same all over the world. (T)

5. A baby's first words are usually words that he or she invents. (T)

6. A child uses only vocabulary and no grammar before about two years of age. (F   He/she actually uses a kind of grammar in making two-word sentences at about 18 months of age.)

7. Children probably say "I goed" instead of "I went" because they hear their parents say this. (F   Children say "I goed" instead of "I went" because they are overgeneralizing the grammar rule for the regular past tense verbs to the irregular verb "go.")

B. The Listening Expansion

TASK 1.

Solving a Word Problem

You are alone in a room. There are two pieces of string hanging from the ceiling. The strings are six feet long and ten and a half feet apart. The only other things in the room are a chair, some pins, some pieces of paper, and a pair of pliers. You job is to tie the two ends of the string together. You may not pull them loose from the ceiling. How will you tie them together?

Solution: Tie the pliers to the end of one of the strings. Start the string swinging in the direction of the other string. Take hold of the end of the other string. You will be able to move close enough to catch the end of the other string when it swings towards you. (You cannot solve the problem by standing on the chair.)

TASK 2.

Explaining Steps in Problem Solving

Take the piece of paper and draw three circles on it. Label the three circles one, two, and three. Okay, now you should have a piece of paper with three circles, circle number one, circle number two, and circle number three. Now take the three coins of different sizes and put them in the first circle. Put the largest coin on the bottom, the next largest coin on top of the largest coin, and the smallest coin on the top. Okay, now you should have three coins stacked up in the first circle, the largest on the bottom and the smallest one on top. Now here is the problem. You are to move all the coins to the third circle so that the largest coin is still on the bottom and the smallest coin is on the top. Here are the rules: 1. You can move only one coin at a time. 2. Only the top coin can be moved. 3. You cannot put a larger coin on a smaller coin. 4. You may move to any circle. Remember your job is to move all the coins to the third circle so that they are in the same order as they are now in the first circle. Don't forget the rules: move only one coin at a time, move only the top coin, and don't put a larger coin on a smaller coin. Good luck!

Solution: Call the largest coin C, the middle coin B, and the smallest coin A. Call the first circle 1, the second circle 2, and the third circle 3.

1. Move A to 3.

2. Move B to 2.

3. Move A to 2.

4. Move C to 3.

5. Move A to 1.

6. Move B to 3.

7. Move A to 3.

Listening Factoid

Have you ever wondered about what the world's original language was? Or whether children would begin to speak if they never heard language? Well, more than 2,500 years ago, an Egyptian pharaoh asked himself the same questions. He had the idea that children who didn't hear adults speaking any language would begin to speak the world's "original language." So he had two newborn babies of poor parents taken away from them. He gave the babies to a shepherd to take care of. No one was allowed to speak to them. About two years later, the shepherd reported to the pharaoh that the children were making a sound like "bekos." This sound "bekos" sounded like the word for bread in the Phrygian language, so the pharaoh concluded that Phrygian was the original language in the world. There was only one problem with the pharaoh's conclusion. He overlooked the fact that "bekos" sounded very much like the noise that sheep make!

II. The Main Listening Task

A. Initial Listening

Researchers at the University of the Virgin Islands have developed a system of hydroponic aquaculture that is both simple and low cost. The system uses *gravity* to create *recirculating water systems* in which both fish and vegetables are grown. Let me explain how this particular system of hydroponic aquaculture works on the island of St. Croix in the Virgin Islands.

To start with, rainwater is collected in a large 3,000 gallon *tank* on the highest point of land on the island. The tank is so large that it measures about 12 feet in diameter. Once the tank is filled with rainwater, fish are added to the tank and are subsequently raised in the rainwater. So, to repeat, first researchers collect rainwater in a large tank; then they add fish to the tank.

The next step in the process happens in this way. The rainwater collected in the large tank slowly runs out of the bottom of the large fish tank and into another tank. This other tank holds the *waste from the fish*. The water *is* then *filtered,* and after it is filtered, it is passed through a "bio-filter" that contains bacteria. These bacteria convert any harmful ammonia produced in the fish waste into nitrates. The nitrates are then used to feed the plants in the next stage of the process.

After the water has passed the bio-filter, it enters two 100-foot long hydroponic tanks. Just above the 100-foot long tanks of water, plants, in this particular case, lettuce plants, are suspended on *trays*. The plant roots hang in the water. Through the roots, the plants *soak up* or *absorb* the nitrates and other nutrients in the water before the water drains out of these 100-foot long tanks into a large reservoir. The reservoir is located at the lowest point on the island. It is now necessary to get the water from the lowest part of the island back up to the highest point on the island so that the water can recirculate through the process again. How do they get the water from the reservoir back up to the highest point on the island? Well, a *pump* is used to cycle the water back up to the 3,000 gallon fish tank, and then the process starts all over again.

The aquaculture scientists say that this relatively simple system produced about 25,000 heads of lettuce and one ton of fish in a year from one tank. A commercial company would need to have several tanks in order to make the process *profitable*, but the researchers at the University of the Virgin Islands have demonstrated how aquaculture can be used to grow plants without using soil. The process might be able to help some countries that are looking for new methods of food production.

B. Mental Rehearsal and Review of the Talk

Researchers have developed a system of hydroponic aquaculture.
The system uses gravity.
It creates recirculating water systems.
Fish and vegetables are grown in the water systems.
Rainwater is collected in a large 3,000 gallon tank.
The tank is on the highest point of the island.
The tank is 12 feet in diameter.
Fish are added to the water in this large tank.
The rainwater slowly runs out of the bottom of the fish tank into another tank of water.
This other tank holds the waste from the fish.
The waste is filtered out of the water.
The water then passes through a "bio-filter."
The bio-filter contains bacteria.
These bacteria convert ammonia produced by the fish waste into nitrate.
The nitrate is used for plant food.
The water then enters two 100-foot long hydroponic tanks.
Lettuce plants are suspended just above the water on trays.
The plants soak up the nitrates and the other nutrients in the water.
The water then drains out of the tanks into a reservoir.
The reservoir is located at the lowest point on the island.
A pump cycles the water back up to the 3,000 gallon fish tank.
The process starts all over again.
The system produces 25,000 heads of lettuce and one ton of fish in a year.
A commercial company would need several tanks to make the process profitable.
The process might help countries looking for new methods of food production.

C. Consolidation

See II. A.

III. The Postlistening Task

A. The Comprehension Check

1. Recognizing Information and Checking Accuracy

1. What makes the water pass from one tank to another in the hydroponic system described? (d)

2. What does the bio-filter contain to destroy harmful ammonia in the fish waste? (a)

3. How many heads of lettuce can be produced with the system described? (d)

4. The width of the large fish tank described is 12 feet in diameter. (T)

5. The large fish tank is 100 feet long. (F   The tanks with the lettuce, not the fish, are 100 feet long.)

6. The lettuce plants use the nitrates in the water as food. (T)

7. Gravity takes the water from the tank with the lettuce plants above it to the tank with the fish in it. (F   A pump is needed to cycle the water from the tank with the plants above it to the tank with the fish in it.)

B. The Listening Expansion

TASK 1.

Listening to Identify Steps

(The numbers should be read as "number 1," "number 2," etc.)

1. Sit upright with legs extended in front of you. Your back should be straight and your arms should be at your side. (picture d)

2. Now take a breath and raise your arms overhead so that your arms are straight up in the air over your head. (picture b or f)

3. Next breathe out and bend forward with your arms stretched out in front of you. (a)

4. Then take hold of your ankles. (g)

5. Next rest your forehead on your knees. (c)

6. Count to eight. Now breath in as you bring your torso back to an upright position with your arms over your head again. (picture f or b)

7. Breath out as you slowly bring your arms back to your sides. (e)

TASK 2.

Taking Your Pulse

Step 1: Put the middle three fingers of your right hand, or your left hand if you are lefthanded, on your left wrist just above your thumb.

Step 2: Press down a little until you feel your pulse beat.

Step 3: Count the number of beats you feel in thirty seconds and write down the number. Look at a watch with a second hand or ask someone to keep time for you.

Step 4: Now wait a few seconds and repeat step 1 and step 2.

Step 5: If you count around the same number of beats the second time, write down this number also and add the first and second numbers. This is your pulse rate. If you didn't count around the same number of beats the second time, then you should wait a few minutes and repeat steps 1 through 4 again.

Listening Factoid

The jackfruit tree of southern Asia bears the world's largest tree fruits. The fruits can weigh as much as 110 pounds. As many as 250 fruits are produced by a single tree each year. People in India and Sri Lanka eat the fruit fresh or make a syrup out of this large fruit. Would you like to eat the jackfruit?

II. The Main Listening Task

A. Initial Listening

News media are the means or methods, by which people learn what is happening in their city, in their country, and in the world. The news media can be classified into two general *categories*. The categories are print media and electronic media. Print media use written material to communicate news to readers. Electronic media use *air waves* to send news into homes, offices, and public places.

Print media are usually divided into magazines and newspapers. Most newspapers print news daily. *For instance,* the newspaper *The New York Times* is *published* every day of the year. In the United States in 1991, 1,586 daily newspapers were published. Most news magazines are published once a week. There are fewer magazines than newspapers published in the U.S. In 1990, it was reported that 11,239 magazines were published every month.

The electronic media are generally divided into radio and television. Radio news is news that you listen to. In the United States, many radio stations *broadcast* five minutes of news every hour on the hour. Television news is news that you not only listen to, but also watch. In Canada and the United States, for example, many people watch an hour of news on TV at six o'clock in the evening.

In the future, new categories of news media will *develop*. Even today, computers are beginning to influence the *transmission* and *reception* of news. For example, in 1992, many *computer users* in the United States were able to receive information about *events* happening in other parts of the world from computer users in those parts of the world. The users transmitted news via electronic mail over computer networks like *BITNET and INTERNET*. Computer users in the U.S. received personal accounts of the news as it was happening. There is little doubt that technology will continue to influence the transmission and reception of news in the future.

B. Mental Rehearsal and Review of the Talk

News media are the media by which people learn what is happening.
They learn what is happening in their city, country, and the world.
News media can be classified into two categories.
The categories are print media and electronic media.
The print media use written material.
Electronic media use air waves.
The air waves send news into homes, offices, and public places.
Print media are divided into magazines and newspapers.

Most newspapers print news daily.

Most news magazines are published weekly.

Electronic media are divided into radio and television.

You listen to radio news.

Many radio stations broadcast five minutes of news every hour.

You listen to and watch television news.

New categories of news media will develop.

Computers are beginning to influence the transmission of news.

Computers are beginning to influence the reception of news.

Computer users in the U. S. receive information about events happening in other parts of the world from users in those parts of the world.

The users sent news via electronic mail over BITNET and INTERNET.

Computer users receive personal accounts of the news.

Technology will continue to influence the transmission and reception of news.

C. Consolidation

See II. A.

III. The Postlistening Task

A. The Comprehension Check

1. Recognizing Information and Checking Accuracy

1. What do the print media use to communicate the news? (d)

2. What do the electronic media use to broadcast news? (a)

3. What is the *New York Times* an example of? (b)

4. Which of the following print media are published? (d)

5. Which of the following electronic media are broadcast? (a)

6. How many magazines are published weekly in the U. S.? (b)

7. The *New York Times* is published once a day. (T)

8. Radio and television are examples of print media. (F   They are examples of electronic media.)

9. Many Canadians and Americans watch the six o'clock news on TV. (T)

10. There will still be only two general categories of news media in the year 2,000. (F   New categories of news media will develop in the future.)

11. The TV news program *Meet the Press* is an example of a long-running news program. (T)

12. Computer users connected to BITNET or INTERNET can obtain news about events in another part of the world even as those events are happening. (T)

B. The Listening Expansion

TASK 1. **Identifying Different Segments of a News Broadcast**

2. The President and his advisers met with representatives of the major banks to discuss ways to control inflation and government spending.

   What kind of news is this? (It's national news.)

3. Here are the results of tonight's college games:

   Penn State 17
   The University of Arizona 14
   Oregon State University 10
   The University of Washington 7
   UCLA beat San Diego State 33 to 19. Well, that's all the scores that are in at this time. Stay tuned for more (fade out).

   What kind of a report is this? (It's a sports report.)

4. Tomorrow and Saturday are big sale days at Thompson's Furniture Warehouse. All furniture in the store has been marked down 30 percent. This is once-in-a-lifetime opportunity to furnish your home with beautiful, quality furniture, at low, low prices. So come on in to Thompson's Warehouse tomorrow and save (fade out).

   What is this? (It's a commercial.)

5. There was a two-car crash at the intersection of Broadway and 29th Street early this evening. The driver of one of the cars is in critical condition at University Hospital. The passengers in the other car escaped injury. The identity of the injured man is not known at this time.

   What kind of news is this? (It's local news.)

6. Members of the Oil Producing and Exporting Countries are meeting tomorrow in Caracas, Venezuela, to discuss declining oil prices and rising inflation. OPEC members will spend three days in private talks on these subjects.

   What kind of news is this? (It's international news.)

TASK 2. **Rating Restaurants**

Restaurant 2

FRED: Uhmmmm. This spaghetti is great! And the bread is really delicious. How's your meal, Mary?

MARY: It's one of the best meals I've had in a long time. I really don't know how they can serve such good food at these prices. Let's bring the children next time. We can afford to come here more often.

(Good Food/Inexpensive Prices)

Restaurant 3

LAURA: Dave, this is a wonderful restaurant. The chicken à la Kiev is superb. And the wine is fantastic. Oh, I just love dining by candlelight, don't you?

DAVE: Yeah, but just wait until the bill comes!

LAURA: Now, Dave, it's our tenth anniversary. This is a special evening. Let's not talk about money.

DAVE: You're right, but we'll have to eat hamburger for the rest of the month.

LAURA: It's worth it!

(Good Food/Expensive Prices)

Restaurant 4

PAM: Mike, why did you bring me to a place like this on our first date? It's so noisy and crowded.

MIKE: I know it is, but tonight's this 2 for 1 special. We can both have a spaghetti dinner for $5.00. Oh, here's the waiter. Later . . . .

Well, how was the spaghetti?

PAM: I'd rather not say. There's one thing I will say: This is our *last* date.

(Bad Food/Inexpensive prices)

Listening Factoid

One of the longest running and most popular weekly programs on American television is a news program called *60 Minutes*. The show began in 1968 and was listed as the most popular program during the decade of the 1980s. Between 1990 and 1993 it remained the most watched weekly program on American TV in the U.S.

UNIT III CHAPTER 2

II. The Main Listening Task

A. Initial Listening

A tidal wave is a very large and very *destructive* wall of water that *rushes* in from the ocean toward the shore. Many scientists call these waves *tsunami*. In Japanese *tsunami* means "storm wave." But do you know that tidal waves are not caused by *storms* and that they are not true tides at all? A true tide is the regular rise and fall of ocean waters, at definite times each day, but a tidal wave comes rushing in suddenly and unexpectedly. A tidal wave is caused by an underwater earthquake. Scientists call the underwater earthquake a seaquake. The word "seaquake" is made up of two words, the word "sea" which means "ocean" and the word "quake." "To quake" means "to shake" or "to tremble." When a seaquake takes place at the bottom of the ocean, the ocean floor shakes and trembles, and sometimes the ocean floor *shifts.* It is this shifting that produces the tidal wave. The tidal wave begins to move across the sea at great speed.

Tidal waves have taken many human lives in the past. Today scientists can *predict* when a tidal wave will hit land. They use a seismograph to do this. A seismograph is an instrument that records the strength, the direction, and the length of time of an earthquake or seaquake. It is not possible to hold back a tidal wave, but it is possible to *warn* people that a tidal wave is coming. This warning can save many lives.

B. Mental Rehearsal and Review of the Talk

A tidal wave is a very large wall of water.
It is a very destructive wall of water.
It rushes in from the ocean toward the shore.
Many scientists call these waves *tsunami.*
Tsunami is a Japanese word.
It means "storm wave."
Tidal waves are not caused by storms.
They are not true tides.
A true tide is the regular rise and fall of ocean water.
A true tide rises and falls at definite times each day.
A tidal wave comes rushing in suddenly and unexpectedly.
It is caused by an underwater earthquake.
An underwater earthquake is called a seaquake.
The word "seaquake" is made up of two words.
The word "sea" means "ocean."
"To quake" means "to shake" or "to tremble."
During a seaquake the ocean floor shakes and trembles.
The ocean floor also sometimes shifts.

The shifting causes the tidal wave.
The tidal wave moves across the sea.
It moves at great speed.
Tidal waves have taken many lives in the past.
Today scientists can predict when a tidal wave will hit land.
They use a seismograph.
A seismograph records the strength and the direction of a seaquake.
It also records the length of time of a seaquake.
It is not possible to hold back a tidal wave.
It is possible to warn people that a tidal wave is coming.
This warning can save many lives.

C. Consolidation

See II.A.

III. The Postlistening Task

A. The Comprehension Check

1. Recognizing Information and Checking Accuracy

2. They can predict when a tidal wave will hit land. (c)

3. It is caused by a seaquake. (d)

4. It is a synonym for "underwater earthquake." (b)

5. During a seaquake, it shakes, trembles, and sometimes shifts. (e)

6. It records the strength, the direction, and the length of time of earthquakes. (f)

B. The Listening Expansion

TASK 1. **Filling In Information and Answering Questions**

1 Down	It's a word with 5 letters. It means a heavy fall of rain or snow with much wind.
10 Down	It's a word with 7 letters. It's what scientists do when they say a tidal wave will hit land.
15 Across	It's a 5-letter word that is plural. These result from the motion of ocean water and are sometimes very large.
25 Across	It's a 10-letter word that begins with the letter "S." They're people who collect and study scientific information.
25 Down	It's a 3-letter word. It's a synonym for the word "ocean."
30 Down	It's a 4-letter word. It's the regular rise and fall of the ocean at different times each day.
37 Across	It's a 4-letter word that begins with the letter "W." It's what scientists do when they tell people that they are in danger.

Crossword grid (answers):

1 S	2 E	3 I	4 S	5 M	6 O	7 G	8 R	9 A	10 P	11 H
12 T									13 R	
14 O					15 W	16 A	17 V	18 E	19 S	
20 R								21 D		
22 M								23 I		
								24 C		
	25 S	26 C	27 I	28 E	29 N	30 T	31 I	32 S	33 T	34 S
	35 E					36 I				
37 W	38 A	39 R	40 N			41 D				
						42 E				

TASK 2.

Catching and Correcting Mistakes in Information

Shortly after noon today a severe earthquake struck the northwestern coast of Japan. A group of about 50 people, including 43 schoolchildren, were caught in a tidal wave that hit the coast 30 minutes after the earthquake. The children had just left their school bus and were headed toward the beach for a seashore picnic. At that moment a 12-foot-high tidal wave hit the beach. The wave carried the children out to sea. At this time 13 children are reported missing.

It is further reported that the quake also caused fires in an oil refinery and widespread destruction of homes. The Prime Minister of Japan has declared a state of emergency in the areas hit by the quake and tidal wave. There will be further details on tonight's six o'clock news.

1. Fifteen people were caught in the tidal wave. (Fifty people were caught in the tidal wave.)

2. The tidal wave hit the coast an hour after the earthquake. (The tidal wave hit the coast 30 minutes after the earthquake.)

3. A 20-foot-high wave struck the beach. (A 12-foot-high wave struck the beach.)

4. The quake caused widespread destruction of beaches. (The quake caused widespread destruction of homes.)

5. The President of the United States declared a state of emergency. (The Prime Minister of Japan declared a state of emergency.)

Listening Factoid

The largest wave was not a *tsunami*. It was caused by a landslide that sent about 100 million tons of rock crashing into a bay in Alaska in 1958. The slide produced a single wave which covered the hills on the opposite side of the bay up to a distance of nearly 1,700 feet inland. Then the wave, which was 200-feet high, raced back out to sea. No one was killed.

II. The Main Listening Task

A. Initial Listening

Imagine rainwater more acid than lemon juice! Imagine forests and lakes dying and *historical monuments* being destroyed by rain. Not just by normal rainwater but by acid rain. Just what is acid rain? Did you know that normal rainwater is already a little acidic? So what makes acid rain different from normal rainwater? Well, the term acid rain actually refers to any form of precipitation, that is, any form of rain or snow, that is **more** acidic than normal rainwater. Let me repeat that definition for you. Acid rain is any form of precipitation that is **more** acidic than normal rainwater. This definition is rather unscientific. So let me give you another, more scientific way of saying what acid rain is. In scientific terms, acid rain is defined as any form of precipitation which has a pH of less than 5.5. The term pH is a term used in chemistry to indicate how acid or how alkaline a solution is. If a solution is neither acid nor alkaline, we say that it is a neutral solution and that it has a pH of 7. If a solution has a pH of less than seven, we say the solution is acidic. So you can see that with a pH of 5.5, normal rainwater is already *slightly acidic*. Ordinary rainwater is slightly acidic because there are some normal gases such as carbon dioxide in the atmosphere. Carbon dioxide is the gas that all animals, including humans exhale. When these gases dissolve in water, they make the water somewhat acidic. So it is perfectly natural that rainwater is a little acidic. But as you heard, today in parts of Europe and North America rainwater is sometimes more acidic than lemon juice.

What causes this rainwater to be so acidic? The most important cause of the excessive acidity of rainwater has been the burning of *fossil fuels* such as petroleum and coal. Burning fossils fuels produces not only carbon dioxide, but also gases such as nitrogen oxide and sulfur dioxide, which go high into the atmosphere. These gases *combine with* water molecules and form acid. These acidic *water droplets* then can travel hundreds of miles before they return to earth as rain or snow.

This will not be an easy problem to solve. As more and more countries become industrialized, there will be more and more *competition* for petroleum for cars, home heating, and industry. While burning petroleum *contributes* greatly to acid rain, it is less polluting than coal. Unfortunately, petroleum is more expensive than coal and the supply of petroleum will eventually run out. Therefore, there will be more and more *pressure* to burn coal for energy. Coal is a much dirtier energy source than petroleum. Since we already know how destructive acid rain is, it's very important that we increase our efforts to find a non-polluting source of energy as quickly as possible, so that we can avoid further environmental damage.

B. Mental Rehearsal and Review of the Talk

Imagine rainwater more acid than lemon juice.
Imagine forests and lakes dying.
Imagine historical monuments being destroyed by rain.
What is acid rain?
Acid rain refers to any form of precipitation that is more acidic than normal rainwater.
Precipitation is any form of rain or snow.
In scientific terms, acid rain is any form of precipitation with a pH of less than 5.5.
The term pH refers to how acid or alkaline a solution is.
A neutral solution has a pH of 7.
A pH of 7 means a solution is neither acid nor alkaline.
Normal rainwater has a pH of 5.5.
Normal rainwater is slightly acidic.
Normal gases such as carbon dioxide are in the atmosphere.
Carbon dioxide is the gas that humans and other animals exhale.
Carbon dioxide is dissolved in water.
This makes normal rainwater slightly acidic.
But today some rainwater is more acidic than lemon juice!
What causes rainwater to be so acidic?
The most important cause has been the burning of fossil fuels.
Fossils fuels are fuels such as petroleum and coal.
Burning fossil fuels produces carbon dioxide and other gases such as nitrogen oxide and sulfur dioxide.
These gases go high up into the atmosphere.
These gases combine with water molecules and form acid.
These acidic water droplets travel many miles.
These water droplets then return to earth as rain or snow.
This will not be an easy problem to solve.
More and more countries are become industrialized.
There will be more and more competition for petroleum for cars, home heating, and industry.
Burning petroleum contributes greatly to acid rain.
Petroleum is more expensive than coal.
There will be more pressure to burn coal.
Coal is dirtier to burn than petroleum.
Acid rain is very destructive to our environment.
We must find a non-polluting source of energy as quickly as possible.

C. Consolidation

See II.A.

III. The Postlistening Task

A. The Comprehension Check

1. Recognizing Information and Checking Accuracy

1. If a solution has a pH of 8, how can we describe the solution? (c)

2. What is the pH of normal rainwater? (b)

3. How can acid rain be scientifically defined? (d)

4. What does the burning of fossil fuels produce? (d)

5. Carbon dioxide is not normally present in the atmosphere. (F   Carbon dioxide is the gas exhaled by all animals and, therefore, is naturally present in the atmosphere.)

6. A neutral solution is a solution with a pH of 7. (T)

7. It would be better if more countries started burning coal instead of petroleum. (F   Burning coal is more polluting than burning petroleum.)

8. As more and more countries become industrialized, there will be more pressure to burn coal. (T)

B. The Listening Expansion

TASK 1.   **Reconstructing Acronyms and Initialisms**

1. Thank God, it's Friday. (I)

2. World Health Organization (I)

3. unidentified flying object (I)

4. Environmental Protection Agency (I)

5. gross national product (I)

6. Organization of Petroleum Exporting Countries (A)

7. National Aeronautics and Space Administration (A)

8. extra-sensory perception (I)

9. acquired immune deficiency syndrome (A)

Answers:
a. 8
b. 4
c. 6
d. 2
e. 1
f. 5
g. 7
h. 3
i. 9

TASK 2.   **Listening to Match a Question With Its Answer**

1. What is the Eiffel Tower? (3)

2. Who was Thomas Edison? (7)

3. What is rice? (4)

4. What are the pyramids? (5)

5. What is the Grand Canyon? (2)

6. Who was Pablo Picasso? (8)

7. What is the Statue of Liberty? (9)

8. Who was Beethoven? (1)

9. What is wheat? (6)

10. What is corn? (10)

Listening Factoid

Everybody knows that automobiles cause a lot of air pollution. We can see smog in every large city of the world. But do you know that there are other motor-driven machines which produce even more smog-producing emissions? For example, a motor-driven lawnmower produces two and a half times as much smog-producing emissions as an automobile, a chain saw produces ten times as much, and an outboard motor produces an astounding forty times as much!

II. The Main Listening Task

A. Initial Listening

Today I want to talk about levels of language usage. You probably have noticed that people express similar ideas in different ways, depending on the situation they are in. This is very natural. All languages have two general, broad categories, or levels of usage: a formal level and an informal level. English is no exception. I'm not talking about correct and incorrect English. What I'm talking about are two levels of correct English. The difference in these two levels is the situation in which you use a particular level. Formal language is the kind of language you find in textbooks, *reference books* such as encyclopedias, and in business letters. For example, a letter to a university would be in formal style. You would also use formal English in compositions and essays that you write in school. People usually use formal English when they give classroom lectures or speeches and at *ceremonies* such as graduations. We also tend to use formal language in conversations with persons we don't know well or with people we have a formal relationship with, such as professors, bosses, doctors, friends of our parents', strangers, etc. Informal language is used in conversation with *colleagues*, family and friends, and when we write personal notes or letters to close friends, as well as in *diaries*, etc.

Formal language is different from informal language in several ways. However, today I'm going to talk only about a couple of ways. First of all, formal language tends to be more polite. Interestingly, it usually takes more words to be polite. For example, I might say to a friend or family member, "Close the door, please," but to a stranger or someone *in authority* I probably would say "Would you mind closing the door?" or "Excuse me, could you please close the door?" Using words like "could" and "would" makes my request sound more polite, but also more formal. I want to be polite but not **too** formal with my friends and family.

Another difference between formal and informal language is some of the vocabulary. There are some words and phrases that belong in formal language and others that are informal. Let me give you a couple of examples of what I mean. Let's say that I really like soccer. If I'm talking to my friend or colleague I might say "I'm just crazy about soccer!" But if I were talking to my supervisor or a friend of my parents', I would probably say "I really enjoy soccer" or "I like soccer very much." Let's say I'm telling someone some news I heard about the police arresting a criminal. To my friend I might say, "The cops bagged the crook." To my parents' friend I might say "The police arrested the thief."

Although the line between formal and informal language is not always clear and although people are probably less formal today than in the past, it is useful to be aware that these two levels, or categories, do exist. The best way for a nonnative speaker of English to learn the difference is to observe the different ways English speakers speak or write in different situations. Television newscasters, your college professors in class, your doctors in their offices, etc., will usually speak rather formally. However, your classmates, *teammates*, family members, friends, etc. will generally speak in an informal fashion. The difference can be learned over time by observing and *interacting* with native speakers.

B. Mental Rehearsal and Review of the Talk

All languages have two general levels of usage.
These two levels are formal and informal.
Both levels are correct.
They are used in different situations.
Formal English is used in textbooks and reference books.
It is also used in business letters, compositions, and essays.
People use formal English in lectures and speeches at ceremonies.
We tend to use formal English with people we don't know well.
We use it with people we have formal relationships with.
We usually have formal relationships with professors, bosses, doctors, friends of our parents', and strangers.
Informal English is used with colleagues, family, and friends.
Informal English is used in diaries, personal notes, and letters to friends.
Formal language is different from informal language.
It is different in several ways.
First, formal language is more polite.
It usually takes more words to be polite.
Words like "could" and "would" sound more polite.
Some of the words and phrases in formal and informal English are different.
The phrase "crazy about" is informal for "like very much."
The word "cop" is informal for "police officer."
The line between formal and informal is not completely clear.
The best way for nonnative speakers of English to learn the difference is to observe.
Observe the way different people use English in different situations.
Television newscasters, college professors, and doctors usually speak formally.
Classmates, teammates, family members, and friends usually speak informally.
Learn the difference by observing and interacting with native speakers.

C. Consolidation

See II. A.

III. The Postlistening Task

A. The Comprehension Check

1. Recognizing Information and Checking Accuracy

1. Which of the following are usually written in formal English? (b)

2. Which of the following people do we usually speak to in informal language? (d)

3. Which of the following is the most formal way to make a request? (d)

4. Which of the following should not be in a composition you write in school? (b)

5. It's unusual to find both a formal and an informal level of usage in a language. (F   All languages have two general, broad categories, or levels of usage: formal and informal.)

6. People usually use formal language when they first meet someone. (T)

7. The sentence "Mary is crazy about that music" would be acceptable in conversation between classmates. (T)

8. The best way to learn the difference between formal and informal English is to look up every new word in the dictionary. (F   The best way is to pay attention to how native speakers use language in different situations and to interact with them.)

B. The Listening Expansion

TASK 1.

Labeling the Parts of an Ancient Calculator

An abacus is a simple manual computing device. In other words, it is a simple manual calculator. An abacus can add, subtract, multiply, and divide numbers. The abacus is thousands of years old. The first abacuses were boards covered with sand or dust in which marks could be made. Although an abacus is very simple, it is a powerful and fast calculator which is still widely used in many parts of the world. Let's label the parts of an abacus. Write the labels for the parts of the abacus on the lines on the lower left side of the abacus. Don't write on the lines at the top of the abacus. We'll use those lines later. Let's begin. The outside part of the abacus is called the frame. It has four sides and is usually made of wood. Write the word frame in the space provided. "Frame" is spelled f...r...a...m...e. I'll spell that again, f...r...a...m...e. The next part you should label is called the crossbar. The crossbar goes from one side of the abacus to the other, that is, from the left side to the right side. The crossbar divides the abacus into two parts, the upper part and the lower part. Label the crossbar. "Crossbar" is spelled c...r...o...s...s...b...a...r. That was c...r...o...s...s...b...a...r. An abacus also has a series of rods that go from the top of the frame to the bottom of the frame. Label the rods in the place provided. The word "rod" is spelled r...o...d..., r...o...d. The last part you need to label is the beads. The beads are the round balls on the rods. There are two beads above the crossbar and five beads below. Label the beads. The word "bead" is spelled b...e...a...d. Okay, now you have finished labeling the four parts of the abacus. Let's go on.

Each rod has a place value. Let's label the place values for the first four rods. Write these labels on the lines on the top of the abacus. The rod farthest to the right is the "ones" position. Write the word "ones" on the line for the rod that is the farthest to the right. Spell it o...n...e...s. The next rod represents the "tens." Write the word "tens" above this rod, t...e...n...s. The next rod represents the "hundreds." Write the word "hundreds," h...u...n...d...r...e...d...s. The last rod we are going to label today is the "thousands." The word "thousands" is spelled t...h...o...u...s...a...n...d...s. Check your spelling of the words "hundreds" and "thousands," h...u...n...d...r...e...d...s and t...h...o...u...s...a...n...d...s. Now you have finished labeling. Continue to listen to learn a little more about the abacus.

The beads represent numbers. For the "ones" rod, each bead below the crossbar is worth one and each bead above the crossbar is worth five. For the "tens" rod, each bead below the crossbar is worth ten and each bead above the crossbar is worth 50. Now answer this question: How much is each bead below the crossbar on the hundreds-rod worth? (pause) How much is each bead on the hundreds-rod above the crossbar worth? (pause) If you said 100 and 500, you were correct.

Let's see how we would add the numbers 16 and 7. First, we would show the number 16 by moving a one-bead, a five-bead, and a ten-bead towards the center. Next, we would add 7 by moving two one-beads and a five-bead towards the center. Finally, we would change the two five-beads to one ten-bead and then we would have the number 23.

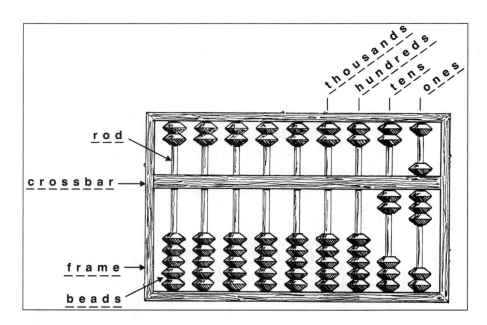

TASK 2.   **Labeling Parts of a Modern Calculator**

Let's begin in the upper right hand corner of the calculator and continue clockwise. That means we will move in the same direction that the hands of a clock move. Are you ready? The first part we will label is the casing. The casing is similar to the frame. Write the word "casing," c...a...s...i...n...g. The next nine parts we will label are different kinds of keys. The word "key" is already labeled to save time. The first key is the clear key: "clear," c...l...e...a...r. The next key is the clear entry key, clear entry key. "Entry" is spelled e...n...t...r...y. The next key is the square root key, square root key. "Square" is spelled s...q...u...a...r...e. "Root" is spelled r...o...o...t. Let's continue moving in a clockwise direction. The next key is called the equals key. "Equals" is spelled e...q...u...a...l...s. The next keys we are going to label are the arithmetic function keys, the arithmetic function keys. "Arithmetic" is spelled a...r...i...t...h-...m...e...t...i...c. "Function" is spelled f...u...n...c...t...i...o...n. Let me repeat those: a...r...i...t...h...m...e...t...i...c and f...u...n...c...t...i...o...n. The next key is the percent key, p...e...r...c...e...n...t. Now label the decimal key. "Decimal" is spelled d...e...c-...i...m...a...l. Now we are ready to label the number entry keys, the number entry keys. You already have the word "entry" you can copy. The word "number" is spelled n...u...m...b...e...r. We're almost finished. We have only three more parts to label. The next keys are the memory function keys, memory function keys. "Memory" is spelled m...e...m...o...r...y. You already have the word "function" you can copy. Now label the display. "Display" is spelled d...i...s...p...l...a...y. Finally, we come to the on/off switch. Write the word "on" to the left of the slash and the word "off" to the right of the slash. "Switch" is spelled s...w...i...t...c...h.

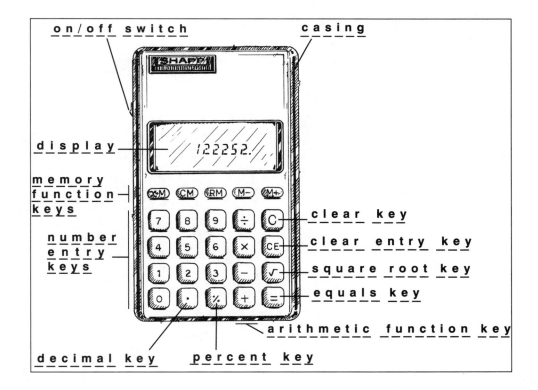

Listening Factoid

The *Oxford English Dictionary*, often referred to as the *OED*, contained 414,825 words when it was finally completed in 1928. The *OED* had been started 71 years earlier. Yes, it took 71 years to complete this dictionary. However, this was not the longest time it ever took to complete a dictionary. One dictionary of the German language took 106 years. Another dictionary of the Italian language was begun in 1863 and still isn't finished.

II. The Main Listening Task

A. Initial Listening

What is power? Psychologists define power as the ability to determine, or to change the actions or *behavior* of other people. Psychologists are trying to identify different kinds of power so that they can better understand how people use these different kinds of power to gain control over other people. They are trying to understand how people *manipulate other people for good* and *evil purposes*. Psychologists have identified five basic types of power, and I'd like to talk about each of these types briefly in the next few minutes.

The first type of power is called *information power*. Some psychologists believe that information power is one of the most effective types of power and control. The person who has information that other people want and need, but do not have, *is in a position of power*. Why is this? Well, most people like to receive and have information. Having information *increases a person's sense of power*. People who provide information can manipulate those who do not have information. Often, when people receive information, they don't know that they *are being manipulated by* those who provided the information. Edwards says, for example, that newspapers provide a lot of information to their readers, and that these newspaper readers generally believe the information they read. Many readers do not question the *accuracy* of the reports about world events they read in the newspapers.

A second types of power is called *referent* power. For example, a person may want to behave like the members of a particular group, such as a soccer team (or a group of classmates), or a person may identify with and want to be like a certain teacher, a friend, or, say, a rock star. If you *identify with* another person, that person has power over you, and that person can influence your actions and behavior. Many people *imitate* and are controlled by the people they identify with. Let me give you a sad example of the use of this type of power for evil purposes. In the 1970s in Jonestown, Guyana, more than 900 people *committed suicide* when their religious leader Jim Jones told them to kill themselves. They did what he told them to do because he had referent power over them. They identified with him; they believed him, and they did what he told them to do. More recently a man named David Koresh controlled the lives and destinies of a small community of men, women, and children in Waco, Texas. Most of them died in a fire with their leader during a confrontation with government agents.

A third kind of power is classified as *legitimate* power. Government officials, according to Edwards, have a lot of legitimate power. When the government decides to raise taxes or make people go to war, most people will do what their government officials tell them to do. One psychologist reported on an experiment that showed an example of this type of power. In this experiment, a researcher asked people on the street to move away from a bus stop. When he was dressed as *a civilian*, few people moved away from the bus stop. When the researcher was dressed as *a guard*, most people moved away from the bus stop. The guard's uniform seemed to give the researcher a look of legitimate power.

A fourth kind of power is called *expert* power. An expert is a person who is very skilled in some area, such as sports, or who knows a lot about something, such as computers. Most people *are impressed by* the skills or knowledge of an expert. Some of these "experts" use their skills at playing sports or knowing about computers to gain power and influence—and to gain money, or admiration, according to Edwards. In other words, they use their expertise to gain power.

Finally, *reward* or *coercive* power is used by people who have the power to reward or to punish another person's actions or behavior. Giving a reward will change people's behavior because it offers people *a chance for gain*. Giving a punishment may or may not cause people to do what the powerful person wants them to do, but the changes may not last for a long time. The person who uses coercive power may also have to carefully watch that the less powerful person does, in fact, change his or her actions or behavior.

To sum up then, power may be gained in many ways. It may come from having information that other people want or need; it may come from being a referent for other people's identification and imitation; it may come from having an official, or legitimate, position of authority; it may come from having skill or expertise; or it may come from having the power to reward or punish people. We all exercise one or more of these various kinds of power over other people, and other people will try to exercise one or more of these kinds of power over us throughout our lives.

B. Mental Rehearsal and Review of the Talk

Power is the ability to determine or change the action of other people.
Psychologists want to understand how people use power to control other people.
People use power to manipulate others for good or evil purposes.
There are five basic types of power.
Information power is one of the most effective types of power.
The person who has information that other people want and need is in a position of power.
Having information increases a person's sense of power.
People often don't know they are being manipulated by those who provide information.
Many newspaper readers don't question the accuracy of the world reports they read.
If you identify with another person, that person has power over you.
That person can influence your actions and behavior.
Many people imitate and are controlled by people they identify with.
In Jonestown, Guyana, 900 people committed suicide.
They did this because their leader told them to kill themselves.

Their leader had referent power over them.

In Texas, Koresh controlled the lives and destinies of a community of men, women, and children.

Government officials have legitimate power.

Most people will do what their government officals tell them to do.

An experiment showed an example of legitimate power.

A researcher dressed as a civilian asked people to move away from a bus stop.

The people did not move away.

A researcher dressed as a guard asked them to move away from the bus stop.

When the guard asked them to move away, most people moved away.

The guard's uniform gave the researcher a look of legitimate power.

An expert is a person who is skilled in some area, such as sports.

An expert is a person who knows a lot about something, such as computers.

Some experts use their skills to gain power, influence, money, and admiration.

Reward or coercive power is used to reward or punish people's actions or behavior.

A reward offers people a change for gain.

Giving a punishment may or may not cause people to do what the powerful person wants.

The change in behavior may not last for long when a punishment is given.

Power may be gained in many ways.

Power may come from having information people want or need.

Power may come from being a referent for other people.

Power may come from having a position of authority.

Power may come from having skill or expertise.

Power may come from having the power to reward or punish.

We all exercise one or more of these kinds of power over people.

Other people try to exercise one or more of these kinds of power over us.

C. Consolidation

See II. A.

III. The Postlistening Task

A. The Comprehension Check

1. Recognizing Information and Checking Accuracy

1. According to the speaker, which is one of the most effective types of power? (d)

2. If a teenager wishes to act like a favorite rock singer, which type of power does that singer have over the teenager? (b)

3. Which kind of power may or may not lead to changes that the person in power wants and requires? (a)

4. Some psychologists believe that information power is one of the most effective types of power. (I heard it.)

5. If a young person wants to act like her older sister, the older sister is a referent of identification. (I can infer it.)

6. Jim Jones used power for evil purposes. (I can infer it.)

7. David Koresh and his followers died in a fire. (I heard it.)

8. Napoleon identified with his father who used power well. (I did not hear it and cannot infer it.)

9. Government officials have a lot of legitimate power. (I heard it.)

10–13. Students prepare their own statements about the content of the talk and ask classmates to listen to their statements and to check the appropriate boxes.

B. The Listening Expansion

TASK 1. **Naming the Animal and Naming the Category**

1. This animal can be black, brown, white, gray, or one of many other colors. It's an animal that eats hay. It has a long tail. It was often used for transportation. It's a four-legged animal. What is it? What is it classed as?

   The answer is horse. Write "horse" on the blank in number 1. Underline "vertebrate." Let's go on.

2. It's an animal that lives in the ocean. It is eaten in some parts of the world. It squirts black ink to protect itself from danger. It has eight legs. What is it? What is it categorized as? (octopus/invertebrate)

3. This animal does not live in the ocean. It has wings, and it has antennae on the top of his head. It lives only a short time during the spring and summer. It is a very beautiful and colorful insect. What is it? What is it designated as? (butterfly/invertebrate)

4. This animal lives in the ocean. The animal lives inside a shell. Sometimes a lucky person finds a beautiful pearl inside the animal's shell. It is often served in seafood restaurants. What is it? What is it typed? (oyster/invertebrate)

5. It is a tiny animal. It spins a web. In its web it catches flies and other small insects. Some of these tiny creatures are poisonous. It is an eight-legged creature. What is it? What is it categorized as? (spider/invertebrate)

6. It's a cold-blooded animal. In other words, it needs to warm its body in the sun in cold weather. Some are poisonous. Their bite can kill a person. It has no feet; so it *slithers* along the ground on its stomach. What is it? What is it classed? (snake/vertebrate)

7. It's an animal that is born in the water, but when it's grown, it can breathe air. It hops along the ground. It does not have a tail. Some people like to eat the legs of this small animal. What is it? What is it categorized as? (frog/vertebrate)

TASK 2.

The Five Categories of Vertebrates: Placing the Animal in the Category

1. A *mammal* is a warm-blooded vertebrate that feeds its young with milk from the mother's body.

2. A *bird* is a warm-blooded vertebrate that has feathers and two feet. Instead of arms, a bird has wings.

3. A *fish* is a cold-blooded vertebrate that lives its entire life in water. It has fins instead of arms or feet. It gets oxygen from the water, not the air.

4. A *reptile* is a cold-blooded vertebrate that crawls or moves on its stomach or on small short legs. Reptile babies hatch from eggs with shells.

5. An *amphibian* is a cold-blooded vertebrate that starts its life in water. Later, an amphibian develops lungs to breathe air. Then it can live on land.

Animal	Category
1. parrot	bird
2. elephant	mammal
3. snake	reptile
4. alligator	reptile
5. shark	fish
6. salamander	amphibian
7. owl	bird
8. tuna	fish
9. human being	mammal
10. frog	amphibian

Listening Factoid

A powerful king named Mithradites lived in Asia Minor almost 2,000 years ago. He was so afraid that someone would try to poison him that in order to build up an immunity to poison, he spent many years drinking small amounts of poison. King Mithradites was very successful in building up his immunity to poison. No one was able to poison him. However, his immunity to poison proved to be a problem when he decided to commit suicide in order to avoid being captured by the Roman army. To avoid being captured by the Romans, he tried to commit suicide by drinking poison. Unfortunately, the poison would not work. In the end, one of his slaves killed him with a sword so he could avoid capture. The man of great power was put to death by the man who had no power.

II. The Main Listening Task

A. Initial Listening

The African and the Asian elephants are the largest land animals in the world. They are really *enormous* animals. The African and the Asian elephants are alike, or similar, in many ways, but there are differences between the two types of elephants, too.

What are some of the similarities between the African and the Asian elephant? Well, for one thing, both animals have long noses, called *trunks*. An elephant sometimes uses its trunk like a third hand. Both kinds of elephants use their trunks to pick up very small objects and very large, heavy objects. They can even pick up trees with their trunks. For another thing, both the African and the Asian elephants have very large ears, although the African elephant's ears are considerably larger.

In addition, both animals are intelligent. They can be *trained* to do heavy work. They can also be trained to do *tricks* to entertain people. In other words, they both work for people, and they entertain people also.

As I said before, the African and the Asian elephants are alike in many ways, but they are also quite different, too. Let me explain what I mean. The African elephant is larger and heavier than the Asian elephant. The African male elephant weighs between 12,000 and 14,000 pounds. In contrast, the average Asian male elephant weighs between 7,000 and 12,000 pounds.

Another major difference between the two kinds of elephants is the size of the ears. Asian elephants have smaller ears than the African elephants do. The teeth are different, too. The African elephant has two very large teeth. These teeth are called tusks. The Asian elephant sometimes does not have any tusks—at all. The elephants differ in color, too. The African elephant is dark gray in color while the Asian elephant is light gray. Occasionally an Asian elephant is even white in color! The last big difference between the two elephants is their *temperament*. The Asian elephant is tamer than the African elephant. In other words, the African elephant is much wilder than the Asian elephant. As a result, it is more difficult to train the African elephant to perform tricks to entertain people. That's why the elephants you see in the circus are probably Asian elephants . . . not African elephants.

Yes, there certainly are differences between the African and the Asian elephants, but there is one big similarity between the two animals; they are both fascinating and enormous animals.

B. Mental Rehearsal and Review of the Talk

The African and the Asian elephants are the largest land animals.
The two elephants are alike in many ways.
There are also differences between the elephants, too.
What are the similarities?
Both animals have long noses, called trunks.
An elephant sometimes uses its trunk like a third hand.
Both the African and the Asian elephants have very large ears.
Both animals can be trained to work for man.
Both can be trained to do tricks.
What are the differences?
The African elephant is larger and heavier than the Asian elephant.
The African male elephant weighs between 12,000 and 14,000 pounds.
The average Asian male elephant weighs between 7,000 and 12,000 pounds.
Asian elephants have smaller ears than African elephants.
The African elephant has two very large teeth.
These teeth are called tusks.
The Asian elephant sometimes does not have any tusks.
The African elephant is dark gray in color.
The Asian elephant is light gray.
Occasionally an Asian elephant is even white.
The Asian elephant is tamer than the African elephant.
The African elephant is much wilder than the Asian elephant.
The elephants you see in the circus are probably Asian elephants.

C. Consolidation

See II. A.

III. The Postlistening Task

A. The Comprehension Check

1. Recognizing Information and Checking Accuracy

1. What part of an elephant's body is its trunk? (b)

2. Which animals can be trained to work for man? (c)

3. What is the range of an African male elephant's weight? (c)

4. Which of the following best describes the Asian elephant in comparison with the African elephant? (a)

5. Which is true of both elephants? (d)

6. Elephants use their trunks to pick up both small and large objects. (I heard it.)

7. Elephants enjoy working and doing tricks for people. (I cannot infer it.)

8. African elephants are generally more dangerous than Asian elephants. (I can infer it.)

9. Asian elephants like people more than African elephants do. (I cannot infer it.)

10. Some Asian elephants have tusks. (I can infer it.)

B. The Listening Expansion

TASK 1.

Completing a Sketch

Let me tell you some more differences between my sisters, Alice and Betty. First of all, Betty wears glasses, but Alice does not. Alice has better eyesight than Betty. For another thing, Betty likes to wear a lot of jewelry—you know, necklaces, earrings, and rings. Today she's wearing two necklaces and a pair of earrings. Alice, on the other hand, usually doesn't wear any jewelry except a wedding ring. She wears a wedding ring because she's married. Betty doesn't wear a wedding ring. She's not married. She's single. Alice, however, is a wife and a mother. She has a young baby named Johnnie. Johnnie is asleep in his crib. Can you draw Johnnie asleep in his crib? I'll pause for a minute to let you draw Johnnie sleeping in his crib. Betty doesn't have any children. She does have pets, however. She has a little yellow bird. It's a canary. Draw Betty's canary in its cage. Betty also has a big cat named Brutus. Brutus would probably eat the canary if he could get into the cage. Draw Brutus, but don't draw him near the cage. Alice, unlike Betty, does not like animals in the house. On the other hand, she does like to have plants in the house. She has one very large house plant she especially likes. See the empty flower pot in the picture. Put a large plant into the pot.

There are many other differences between Betty and Alice, but that's all I'll tell you about right now.

TASK 2.

Listening Dictation

1. Both Charles and David work in an office.

2. Both of my brothers are married.

3. Charles has two children, and David does, too.

4. David likes to play golf, and so does Charles.

5. The two of them have very similar lifestyles.

Listening Factoid

In the early 1970s five baby elephants were released in Kruger National Park in South Africa near a herd of buffalo. Park rangers later reported that one of the young elephants had joined the herd of buffalo and was acting like a buffalo. A visitor to the park in 1980 saw the 10-year-old elephant with its adopted family of about 20 buffalo. The buffalo and the elephant were trying to chase some lions away from a water hole. A few years later a park ranger reported seeing the young elephant and the herd of buffalo drinking water from a water hole when a herd of elephants arrived to drink water. The herd of buffalo ran off when they saw the herd of elephants, and the young elephant ran off along with the herd of buffalo. It appears that the elephant was accepted as a member of the herd by the buffalo.

II. The Main Listening Task

A. Initial Listening

John F. Kennedy and Abraham Lincoln lived in different times and had very different family and educational *backgrounds*. Kennedy lived in the 20th *century;* Lincoln lived in the 19th century. Kennedy was born in 1917, whereas Lincoln was born more than a hundred years earlier, in 1809. As for their family backgrounds, Kennedy came from a rich family, but Lincoln's family was not wealthy. Because Kennedy came from a wealthy family, he was able to attend expensive private schools. He graduated from Harvard University. Lincoln, on the other hand, had only one year of *formal schooling.* In spite of his lack of formal schooling, he became a well-known lawyer. He taught himself law by reading law books. Lincoln was, in other words, a self-educated man.

In spite of these differences in Kennedy and Lincoln's backgrounds, some interesting similarities between the two men are evident. In fact, books have been written about the strange *coincidences* in the lives of these two men. For example, take their political careers. Lincoln began his political career as a *Congressman.* Similarly, Kennedy also began his political career as a Congressman. Lincoln was elected to the *U.S. House of Representatives* in 1847, and Kennedy was elected to the House in 1947. They went to Congress just 100 years apart. Another interesting coincidence is that each man was elected President of the United States in a year ending with the number 60. Lincoln was elected President in 1860, and Kennedy was elected in 1960; furthermore, both men were President during years of *civil unrest* in the country. Lincoln was President during the American Civil War. During Kennedy's term of office, civil unrest took the form of *civil rights demonstrations.*

Another striking similarity between the two men was that, as you probably know, neither President lived to complete his term in office. Lincoln and Kennedy were both *assassinated* while in office. Kennedy was assassinated in Dallas, Texas, after only 1,000 days in office. Lincoln was assassinated in 1865 a few days after the end of the American Civil War. It is rather curious to note that both presidents were shot while they were sitting next to their wives.

These are only a few examples of the uncanny—the unusual—similarities in the *destinies* of these two Americans, men who had a tremendous *impact* on the social and political life in the United States and the imagination of the American people.

B. Mental Rehearsal and Review of the Talk

Kennedy and Lincoln lived in different times.

They had different family and educational backgrounds.

Kennedy lived in the 20th century.

Lincoln lived in the 19th century.

Kennedy was born in 1917.

Lincoln was born in 1809.

Kennedy came from a wealthy family.

He went to expensive private schools.

He graduated from Harvard University.

Lincoln had only one year of formal schooling.

He taught himself law and became a lawyer.

He was a self-educated man.

There are many coincidences in the lives of the two men.

Lincoln began his political career as a Congressman.

Kennedy began his political career as a Congressman.

Lincoln was elected to the Congress in 1847

Kennedy was elected to the Congress in 1947.

Lincoln was elected President in 1860.

Kennedy was elected President in 1960.

Lincoln and Kennedy were presidents during years of civil unrest.

Lincoln was President during the Civil War.

During Kennedy's term there were civil rights demonstrations.

Neither lived to complete his presidency.

Lincoln was assassinated in 1865.

Kennedy was assassinated in 1963 in Dallas, Texas.

Kennedy and Lincoln had a tremendous impact on the social and political life of the United States.

They had an impact on the imagination of the American people.

C. Consolidation

See II. A.

III. The Postlistening Task

A. The Comprehension Check

1. Recognizing Information and Checking Accuracy

A variety of answers are possible. Here are some sample responses.

1. In what century was Lincoln born? (the 19th century)

2. Why was Kennedy able to attend expensive private schools? (because his family was rich)

3. How many years did Lincoln attend school? (one year)

4. How did Lincoln get most of his education? (by reading books at home)

5. How did both Kennedy and Lincoln begin their political careers? (as Congressmen; as members of the U. S. House of Representatives)

6. When was Kennedy elected President? (in 1960)

7. During which American war was Lincoln President? (during the American Civil War)

8. How did both Kennedy and Lincoln die? (by assassination; they were assassinated)

9. How long was Kennedy President of the United States? (1,000 days)

10. When was Lincoln murdered? (in 1865; a few days after the end of the Civil War)

B. The Listening Expansion

TASK 1. **A Dictation on Similarities**

1. Both women were 24 years old when they married.

2. Neither of the women was interested in politics.

3. Both were socially prominent women who spoke French.

4. Both Mrs. Lincoln and Mrs. Kennedy suffered the death of a child.

5. Neither Mrs. Kennedy nor Mrs. Lincoln was injured by the assassin.

TASK 2. **Detecting Similarities and Differences.**

1. Andrew Johnson was a large man, and so was Lyndon Johnson. (similarity)

2. Neither of the vice-presidents was from the North. (similarity)

3. Lyndon Johnson was later elected President of the United States, whereas Andrew Johnson was not. (difference)

4. Andrew Johnson had 13 letters in his name, and Lyndon Johnson did, also. (similarity)

5. Kennedy's vice-president was born in the 19th century while Lincoln was born in the 18th century. (difference)

Listening Factoid

Lincoln issued the Emancipation Proclamation during the Civil War. The Proclamation freed the slaves, but only those in the Confederate States. It did not free the slaves living in Kentucky, Maryland, and the other slave-holding states that fought on the side of the North. Why then is Lincoln called "The Great Emancipator"? He deserves to be called "The Great Emancipator" not because of this 1853 proclamation, but because he urged Congress to adopt the Thirteenth Amendment, which abolished slavery in the United States. The amendment was passed by the American Congress in 1865.

II. The Main Listening Task

A. Initial Listening

On the morning of April 12, 1912, the *luxury liner* the *Titanic* left England on a voyage to New York. Four days later she lay at the bottom of the Atlantic Ocean. On Wednesday July 18, 1956, the ocean liner the *Andrea Doria* left Italy. The *Andrea Doria* was also traveling to New York. Eight days later this great ship also lay at the bottom of the Atlantic.

The sinking of these two huge ships, these two very, very large ships, *shocked* the world. Reports of these two *tragedies* filled the newspapers for days. When the *Andrea Doria* went down, people compared her sinking with the sinking of the *Titanic.* There were similarities between the two events; however, there were also important differences.

What were some of these similarities? First of all, both ships were transatlantic ocean liners. In addition, they were also both luxury liners. They carried many of the world's famous and rich people. In fact, ten American millionaires lost their lives when the *Titanic* went down. Today millions of dollars worth of gold, silver, and cash may still remain locked inside these two sunken ships.

Another similarity was that as each ship was sinking, there were acts of *heroism* and acts of *villainy.* Some people acted very bravely, even heroically. Some people even gave up their lives so that others could live. There were also some people who acted like *cowards.* For example, one man on the *Titanic* dressed up as a woman so that he could get into a lifeboat and save his own life. One last similarity was that both of these ships were considered "unsinkable." People believed that they would never sink.

I'd like to shift my attention now to the differences between these great ship *disasters.* To begin with, the *Titanic* was on her maiden voyage; that is, she was on her very first voyage across the Atlantic. The *Andrea Doria,* on the other hand, was on her 101st transatlantic crossing. Another difference was that the ships sank for different reasons. The *Titanic* struck an *iceberg* while the *Andrea Doria collided with* another ship. Another contrast was that the *Andrea Doria* had radar to warn of the approach of another ship, but the *Titanic* was not equipped with radar. The *Titanic* had only a *lookout.* The lookout was able to see the iceberg only moments before the ship struck it. But, of course, the greatest difference between these two terrible accidents was the number of lives lost. When the *Titanic* sank, more than 1,500 people died. They drowned or froze to death in the icy North Atlantic water. Over 700 people *survived* the sinking of the *Titanic.* In the *Andrea Doria* accident 60 people lost their lives, and about 1,650 lives were saved. One of the reasons that so many people died on the *Titanic* was that the ship was considered to be unsinkable, and so there were about half the number of lifeboats needed to *rescue* all the people aboard the ship. The *Andrea Doria* had more than enough lifeboats to rescue every person on the ship; however, they were able to use only about half of the lifeboats they had because of a mechanical problem. The passengers and *crew* of the *Andrea Doria* were very lucky that another ship was able to rescue most of them. The passengers on the *Titanic* were not so fortunate. It is interesting that the wreck of the *Titanic* was only found in September of 1985.

Whenever there are large numbers of people traveling together on a boat, ship, or plane, the possibility of disaster is always present. Most people arrive safely at their destination, but accidents like shipwrecks and plane crashes do happen, and these accidents remind us that no matter how safe we feel, accidents can happen suddenly and unexpectedly.

B. Mental Rehearsal and Review of the Talk

On April 12, 1912, the *Titanic* left England.
The *Titanic* left for New York.
Four days later she was at the bottom of the ocean.
On July 18, 1956, the *Andrea Doria* left Italy.
She was also traveling to New York.
Eight days later she was at the bottom of the Atlantic.
The sinking of these two ships shocked the world.
Reports filled the newspapers for days.
People compared the *Andrea Doria* with the *Titanic*.
There were similarities between the two events.
There were also differences.
What were the similarities?
Both were transatlantic ocean liners.
Both were luxury liners.
They carried many rich, famous people.
Millions of dollars remain inside the ships.
There were acts of heroism and villainy.
Both ships were considered unsinkable.
There were differences between the ship disasters.
The *Titanic* was on her maiden voyage.
The *Andrea Doria* was on her 101st crossing.
The ships sank for different reasons.
The *Titanic* struck an iceberg.
The *Andrea Doria* collided with another ship.
The *Andrea Doria* had radar.
The *Titanic* had only a lookout.
There was a difference in the number of lives lost.
More than 1,500 people died on the *Titanic.*
Over 700 people survived.
Sixty people died on the *Andrea Doria.*
One thousand six hundred fifty lives were saved.
There were about half the needed lifeboats on the *Titanic.*
The *Andrea Doria* had enough lifeboats.

But they were able to use only half of the lifeboats.
Another ship rescued most of the passengers and crew.
Whenever people travel, there is a possibility of disaster.

C. Consolidation

See II. A.

III. The Postlistening Task

A. The Comprehension Check

1. Recognizing Information and Checking Accuracy

1. What was the destination of the *Titanic* as it was sailing across the Atlantic? (c)

2. How were the *Titanic* and the *Andrea Doria* similar? (d)

3. How were the *Titanic* and the *Andrea Doria* different? (b)

4. Dressing up as a woman to save your life is an example of which of the following? (c)

5. What was different about the sinking of the *Andrea Doria* from the sinking of the *Titanic?* (b)

6. Fewer people on the *Titanic* would have died if there had been more lifeboats available. (I can infer it.)

7. The *Andrea Doria* was crossing the Atlantic for the 101st time. (I heard it.)

8. More people on the *Andrea Doria* would have died if there hadn't been another ship near by to rescue most of the people. (I can infer it.)

9. It's very dangerous to travel the Atlantic by ship. (I cannot infer it.)

10. The *Titanic* struck an iceberg, but the *Andrea Doria* collided with another ship. (I heard it.)

11. The radar system on the *Andrea Doria* was not working when the two ships collided. (I cannot infer it.)

B. The Listening Expansion

TASK 1. **A Dramatization**

SS: Did you hear any cries of distress?

OP: Oh, yes.

SS: What were they—cries for help?

OP: Crying, shouting, moaning.

SS: From the ship or from the water?

OP: From the water after the ship disappeared—no noises before . . . .

SS: Did you attempt to get near them?

OP: As soon as she disappeared, I said "Now, men, we will pull toward the wreck." Everyone in my boat said it was a mad idea, because we had far better save what few we had in my boat than go back to the scene of the wreck and be swamped by the crowds that were there.

SS: Tell us about your fellow passengers on that lifeboat. You say they discouraged you from returning or going in the direction of these cries?

OP: They did. I told my men to get their oars out and pull toward the wreck—the scene of the wreck . . . I said, "We may be able to pick up a few more."

SS: Who demurred to that?

OP: The whole crowd in my boat. A great number of them did.

SS: Women?

OP: I couldn't discriminate whether women or men. They said it was rather a mad idea.

SS: I'll ask you if any woman in your boat appealed to you to return to the direction from which the cries came.

OP: No one.

SS: You say that no woman passenger in your boat urged you to return?

Charles Burlingham interrupts: It would have capsized the boat, Senator.

SS: Pardon me. I am not drawing any unfair conclusion from this. One of the officers told us that a woman in his boat urged him to return to the side of the ship. I want to be very sure that this officer heard no woman asking the same thing. Who demurred, now that you can specifically recall?

OP: I could not name anyone in particular.

SS: The men with the oars?

OP: No, they did not. No. They started to obey my orders.

SS: You were in command. They ought to have obeyed your orders.

OP: So they did.

SS: They did not—if you told them to pull toward the ship.

OP: They commenced pulling toward the ship, and the passengers in my boat said it was a mad idea on my part to pull back to the ship because if I did, we should be swamped with the crowd that was in the water, and it would add another forty to the list of the drowned. And I decided I wouldn't pull back . . . .

SS:	How many of these cries were there?
OP:	I'd rather you didn't speak about that.
SS:	I would like to know how you were impressed by it.
OP:	Well, I can't very well describe it. I'd rather you not speak of it.
SS:	I realize that it isn't a pleasant theme, and yet I would like to know whether these cries were general and in a chorus or desultory and occasional?
OP:	There was a continual moan for about an hour.
SS:	And you lay in the vicinity of that scene for about an hour?
OP:	Oh, *please,* sir, don't! I cannot bear to recall it. I wish we might not discuss the scene!
SS:	I have no desire to lacerate your feelings. But we must know whether you drifted in the vicinity of that scene for about an hour.
OP:	Oh, yes, we were in the vicinity of the wreck the whole time . . . .
SS:	Did this anguish or these cries of distress die away?
OP:	Yes, they did—they died away gradually.
SS:	Did they continue during most of the hour?
OP:	Oh, yes—I think so. It may have been a shorter time—of course I didn't watch every five minutes!
SS:	I understand that, and I am not trying to ask about a question of five minutes. Is that all you care to say?
OP:	I'd rather you'd have left that out altogether.
SS:	I know you would, but I must know what efforts you made to save the lives of passengers and crew under your charge. If that is all the effort you made, say so and I will stop that branch of my examination.
OP:	That is all, sir! That's all the effort I made.

TASK 2.

Deciding Whether You Agree or Disagree With Stated Opinions

1. Senator Smith thought that Officer Pitman should have gone back for more people who were still in the water.

2. If Officer Pitman had gone back for the people in the water, he would have been putting the people already in his boats in danger.

3. Officer Pitman made the right decision not to go back for the people in the water.

4. Senator Smith was not sympathetic to Officer Pitman.

5. Officer Pitman was telling the truth.

6. It was the fault of the women on the boat that Officer Pitman did not go back to pick up the people in the water.

7. Officer Pitman was not sure that he had made the right decision not to return to pick up more people.

8. Officer Pitman was still very upset by what had happened.

9. You would have acted differently if you had been Officer Pitman.

10. It's difficult for anyone to know how he or she would act in a terrible situation like the sinking of the *Titanic.*

11. Officer Pitman acted like a villain and a coward.

Listening Factoid

In a recent survey reported in the Pittsburgh *Post-Gazette,* American men were asked if they would give up their seats to other people if they were on the *Titanic* today. Seventy-four percent of the men said they would give up their seat in a lifeboat for their child. Almost as many men, 67%, said they would surrender their seat to their wife. Fifty-four percent reported that they would give their seat to their mother, and 52% said they would for their father. Only 35% said they would give up their seat to any other woman who was not a wife or a child. However, 52% said they would give up their seat for the Catholic humanitarian Mother Teresa, but only 8% said they would give up their seat to pop singer Madonna.

II. The Main Listening Task

A. Initial Listening

The American Civil War was fought over 100 years ago. It began in 1861 and lasted until 1865. The American Civil War resulted in the death of 800,000 Americans. What caused this terrible civil war between the North and the South?

Well, historians believe that there were many causes of the war. One of the important causes of the war was the *friction* between the North and the South over the issue of slavery. The southern way of life and the southern economy were based on the use of slave labor. For almost 250 years before the Civil War, the economy of the South depended on the use of black slaves. The slaves were used to plant and pick cotton and tobacco. Cotton and tobacco were the main crops grown in the South. Most Southerners did not think it was wrong to own, buy, or sell black slaves like farm animals. Slavery was, in fact, the *foundation* of the entire economy and way of life in the South. This was not the situation in the North. The northern economy did not depend on the use of slave labor. Why not?

Well, in the South there were many large cotton *plantations* that used hundreds of black slaves. In the North, however, there were smaller farms. The northern farmers planted many different kinds of crops, not just cotton or tobacco. The Northerners did not need slaves since their farms were smaller than most of the southern plantations. In fact, many Northerners were so opposed to slavery that they wanted to end slavery completely. The northern *attitude* against slavery made the Southerners angry. So, for many years before the war there was constant friction between the North and the South over this issue. This friction eventually led to war.

There was other friction, too, as I said before, between the North and the South. There were, in other words, other causes of *conflict* between the North and the South. One involved the growth of industry in the North. While the South remained an agricultural area, the North became more and more industrialized. As industry increased in the North, it brought more people and greater wealth to the northern states. As a result, many Southerners began to fear northern political and economic *domination*. Because of this fear, many Southerners believed that the South should leave *the Union* and that they should form their own country.

In 1860, the Southerners decided it was time to leave the Union when Abraham Lincoln became President of the United States. Lincoln, as you may know, was against slavery. The people of the South were afraid that their way of life and their economic system were in danger with Lincoln in the Presidency. Consequently, the southern states decided to *secede* from the Union. In other words, they wanted to break away from the North and form a separate country. In 1861, South Carolina seceded, and by June of 1861 eleven southern states had seceded and established a new country. They called the new country the *Confederate States of America*. The war between the North and the South began when the southern states seceded from the Union.

The main reason that the North went to war against the South was to bring the southern states back into the Union. In other words, the North went to war to keep the United States one country.

After four years of terrible fighting, the North won the war against the South, and the United States remained one country. The North won the war mainly because of its economical and industrial strength and power.

The Civil War had two important results for the United States: (1) the Civil War *preserved* the United States as one country; and (2) it ended slavery in the United States.

Many Americans wonder what the United States would be like today if the South had won the Civil War. The history of the United States would have been very different if the South had won the war between the States.

B. Mental Rehearsal and Review of the Talk

The American Civil War was fought over 100 years ago.
The Civil War began in 1861.
The war lasted until 1865.
The war resulted in the death of about 800,000 Americans.
What caused the Civil War between the North and the South?
There were many causes of the war.
One cause was the issue of slavery.
The southern way of life was based on slave labor.
The economy of the South depended on black slaves for 250 years.
Slaves planted and picked cotton and tobacco.
Southerners owned, bought, and sold black slaves.
Southerners did not think this was wrong.
Slavery was the foundation of the southern economy.
The northern economy did not depend on slave labor.
In the South, there were many large cotton plantations.
These plantations used hundreds of black slaves.
In the North, there were smaller farms.
The northern farmers planted many different crops.
Northerners did not need slaves on their small farms.
Many Northerners were opposed to slavery.
Many Northerners wanted to end slavery completely.
The northern attitude against slavery made Southerners angry.
There was constant friction between the North and the South.
The friction was over the issue of slavery.
The friction eventually led to war.
There were other frictions between the North and the South.

One friction involved the growth of industry in the North.
The South remained an agricultural area.
The North became more and more industrialized.
Industry brought people and wealth to the North.
Southerners began to fear northern political and economic domination.
Many Southerners wanted to leave the Union.
The Southerners wanted to form a separate country.
In 1860, Abraham Lincoln became President.
Lincoln was against slavery.
The southern states decided to secede from the Union.
In 1861, South Carolina seceded.
By June of 1861 eleven southern states had seceded.
The eleven southern states established a new country.
The new country was called the Confederate States of America.
The Civil War began when the southern states seceded from the Union.
The North went to war to bring the southern states into the Union.
After four years, the North won the war.
The North won the war because of its economic and industrial power.
The Civil War had two important results.
The Civil War preserved the United States as one country.
The Civil War ended slavery in the United States.
American history might have been different if the South had won.

C. Consolidation

See II. A.

III. The Postlistening Task

A. The Comprehension Check

1. Recognizing Information and Checking Accuracy

1. How long did the American Civil War last? (b)

2. What was one cause of the American Civil War? (b)

3. Describe the economy of the South at the time of the Civil War. (c)

4. How was the economy of the North different from the economy of the South before the war? (d)

5. How did the growth of industry change the North? (b)

6. Why did the South decide to leave the Union and form its own country? (b)

7. What was the name of the country formed by the southern states? (d)

8. What was the most important reason that the North went to war with the South? (b)

9. Why did the North win the war? (d)

10. What did the Civil War accomplish? (c)

1. The American Civil War started in 1861. (T)

2. The American Civil War ended over 100 years ago. (T)

3. There were many large cotton plantations in the North before the war. (F   There were many large cotton plantations in the South.)

4. The use of slaves in the South began around the time of the American Civil War. (F   For almost 250 years before the Civil War, the economy of the South depended on the use of slaves.)

5. Most Southerners felt that it was all right to own, buy, and sell slaves. (T)

6. Most slaves were unhappy and wanted President Lincoln to free them. (?)

7. Most Northerners wanted to use slaves to work on their small farms. (F   The Northerners did not need slaves on their small farms.)

8. The only reason for the American Civil War was the issue of slavery. (F   There were other causes of the conflict between the North and the South, for example, the growth of industry in the North.)

9. The North had better soldiers and generals than the South did. (?)

10. The American Civil War was over in a few months. (F   The war lasted from 1861 to 1865.)

B. The Listening Expansion

TASK 1. **A Listening Dictation**

1. The South lost the war because it had fewer men and far fewer supplies.

2. The South could not ship supplies to its soldiers since it did not have many railroads.

3. The North won the war as a result of its industrial power.

4. The soldiers of the South suffered because of a lack of food.

5. The greater number of soldiers in the North was due to the fact that it had a larger population.

TASK 2. **Guessing Possible Causes of Events**

2. A foreign student has just arrived at L.A. International Airport. He is waiting at the place were the luggage arrives. He has been waiting for a long time. He still hasn't seen his suitcases. What are some possible reasons he has not been able to find his luggage?

(Maybe he is waiting at the wrong place. Perhaps his luggage is lost.

His luggage might be a little late arriving. Maybe he doesn't recognize his bags. Somebody might have taken his luggage by mistake. It's possible that someone has stolen his bags, etc.)

3. A man has just come home from work. He doesn't say hello to his wife. He goes directly into the living room and turns on the TV. He looks very angry. His wife asks him, "What's wrong?" He replies, "Nothing. Leave me alone." Why is the man angry? What happened at work that might have upset the man?

(Maybe he had a fight with his boss or one of his coworkers. He is very tired today and just wants to rest before dinner. The traffic on the way home was terrible. He got fired from his job. He is angry with his wife because . . . .)

4. Professor Jones is lecturing to her class. Suddenly she stops talking. She goes to the window and opens it. She stands at the window for a few minutes. Then she turns and leaves the room very quickly. She doesn't say anything to her students, but the door slams loudly when she leaves the room. Two students who were sleeping in the back of the room wake up and are very surprised that the professor has left. What are some possible reasons for the professor's behavior?

(The professor is sick. She saw something outside the building that she needed to do something about. What could that be? She is angry with the students that were sleeping in class, etc.)

5. You see a man in front of an expensive jewelry store in a large city. He is walking back and forth in front of the store. He looks into the store when he passes the door. From time to time he looks at his watch. He looks up and down the street nervously. He appears very upset. What are some possible causes for his nervousness?

(He is waiting for someone who is late. He can't decide if he wants to go into the store to buy his wife an expensive piece of jewelry or not. He is planning to rob the store and he's waiting for a good time to do it, etc.)

6. Your roommate has just opened a letter from home. She reads the letter, drops it on the floor, and starts to laugh and dance around the room. Why is she so happy?

(Her family sent her money to return home for a short vacation. Someone in her family is coming to visit her. One of her family or friends has had some good fortune. What is it?)

Listening Factoid

In 1853, a very important book against slavery was written by a woman who hated slavery. Her name was Harriet Beecher Stowe, and the title of the book was *Uncle Tom's Cabin*. The book quickly sold 100,000 copies; it helped create a wave of hatred against slavery in the North. When asked why she wrote it, Stowe stated that she had not written the book. She said, "God wrote it. I merely wrote His dictation." *Uncle Tom's Cabin* contributed to the start of the Civil War between the North and the South. In fact, when Abraham Lincoln met Harriet Beecher Stowe, he asked, "Is this the little woman whose book made such a great war?"